D1432897

REMEMBERING DR. PETER L. BENSON (1946–2011)

Dr. Peter L. Benson, former President and CEO of Minneapolis-based Search Institute, was one of the world's leading authorities on positive human development. Dr. Benson's international reputation emerged in the 1990s through his innovative research-based framework of the Developmental Assets. His vision, research, and public voice inspired a "sea change" in research, practice, and policy, shifting away from trying to "fix" what's wrong with kids, toward identifying and building on kids' strengths.

Dr. Benson was 65 years old when he died in 2011. His accomplishments were significant, including his work as the author or editor of more than a dozen books on child and adolescent development and social change. He co-authored *What Kids Need to Succeed*, which has sold more than 800,000 copies. His other books include *Parent, Teacher, Mentor, Friend; Vision: Awakening Your Potential to Create a Better World; Sparks: How Parents Can Ignite the Hidden Strengths of Teenagers;* and *All Kids Are Our Kids: What Communities Must Do to Raise Caring and Responsible Children and Adolescents (2nd Edition).*

"What an absolutely fabulous book! . . . Martha Roper—one of the nation's best and most experienced health educators—has translated her 40 years of teaching into a highly accessible and practical guide, seamlessly leading the reader through the theory and everyday practice of helping young people learn about their sexuality. The reader benefits from her wide classroom experiences with students, colleagues, parents, and administrators. . . . Even the most experienced teacher will learn from her inspired lesson plans."

Robert Selverstone, Ph.D., former board chair of SIECUS

"Teachers, new or seasoned, need this book! If you teach at a public or private school, if you teach health, a family or advisory class, or need a lesson meaningful to students between units, this is the book! Not only are lessons accessible, but the book also provides important, useful, and respectful contexts for the lessons."

Judith Steinhart, Ed.D., health and sexuality teacher and consultant, and co-creator of Columbia University's *Go Ask Alice!*

Healthy Teen Relationships

Using Values & Choices to Teach Sex Education

MARTHA R. ROPER

THREE RIVERS PUBLIC LIBRARY
MINOOKA BRANCH
109 N. WABENA AVE.
MINOOKA, IL 60447
815-467-1600

SEARCH
INSTITUTE
PRESS

Healthy Teen Relationships: Using Values and Choices to Teach Sex Education
Martha R. Roper

Copyright © 2011 by Search Institute

The following are registered trademarks of Search Institute: Search Institute®, Developmental Assets®, and HC • HY®.

All rights reserved. No parts of this publication may be reproduced in any manner, mechanical or electronic, without prior permission from the publisher except in brief quotations or summaries in articles or reviews, or as individual activity sheets for educational use only. For additional permission, write to Permissions at Search Institute.

At the time of publication, all facts and figures cited herein are the most current available; all telephone numbers, addresses, and website URLs are accurate and active; all publications, organizations, websites, and other resources exist as described in this book; and all efforts have been made to verify them. The authors and Search Institute make no warranty or guarantee concerning the information and materials given out by organizations or content found at websites that are cited herein, and we are not responsible for any changes that occur after this book's publication. If you find an error or believe that a resource listed herein is not as described, please contact Client Services at Search Institute.

10 9 8 7 6 5 4 3 2 1
Printed on acid-free paper in the United States of America

Search Institute
615 First Avenue Northeast, Suite 125
Minneapolis, MN 55413
www.search-institute.org
612-376-8955 • 877-240-7251, ext. 1

ISBN-13: 978-1-57482-287-8

Credits
Editor: Kate Brielmaier
Book Design: Jeenee Lee
Production Supervisor: Mary Ellen Buscher

Library of Congress Cataloging-in-Publication Data
Roper, Martha R.
  Healthy teen relationships : using values and choices to teach sex education / Martha R. Roper.
    p. cm.
Includes index.
ISBN-13: 978-1-57482-287-8
  (pbk. : alk. paper)
ISBN-10: 1-57482-287-X (pbk. : alk. paper)
1. Sex instruction for teenagers.
2. Sexual ethics for teenagers.
    I. Title.
HQ35.R67 2011
613.9071—dc23
                              2011027726

Licensing and Copyright
The educational activity sheets in *Healthy Teen Relationships: Using Values and Choices to Teach Sex Education* may be copied as needed. For each copy, please respect the following guidelines:

• Do not remove, alter, or obscure the Search Institute credit and copyright information on any activity sheet.
• Clearly differentiate any material you add for local distribution from material prepared by Search Institute.
• Do not alter the Search Institute material in content or meaning.
• Do not resell the activity sheets for profit.
• Include the following attribution when you use the information from the activity sheets in other formats for promotional or educational purposes: **Reprinted with permission from *Healthy Teen Relationships: Using Values and Choices to Teach Sex Education* by Martha R. Roper [specify the title of the activity sheet you are quoting]. Copyright © 2011 by Search Institute®, Minneapolis, Minnesota, 877-240-7251 ext. 1, www.search-institute.org. All rights reserved.**

Contents

PETER C. SCALES, PH.D.
Senior Fellow, Search Institute

Developmental Assets and Sex Education

Search Institute, a nonprofit research group, has identified 40 protective factors that teens can draw on. The 40 Developmental Assets describe qualities and experiences that are crucial to positive youth development. They range from external supports such as a caring school climate and positive family communication to internal characteristics such as school engagement and a sense of purpose.

Search Institute has done extensive research, reviewing more than 1,200 studies from major bodies of literature, including prevention, resilience, and adolescent development, to identify what young people need to thrive. Institute researchers have documented that young people who are healthy, whether they come from the poorest or the wealthiest environments and from diverse ethnic and cultural groups, have certain meaningful elements in their lives. Researchers identified eight categories that describe these elements:

- The solid presence of **support** from others;
- A feeling of **empowerment**;
- A clear understanding of **boundaries and expectations**;
- Varied opportunities for **constructive use of time**;
- A strong **commitment to learning**;
- An appreciation of **positive values**;
- Sound **social competencies**; and
- A personal sense of **positive identity**.

Moreover, research conducted by Search Institute consistently shows that the strengths described within these categories provide a solid foundation for positive development and academic success, and that their presence helps prevent youth from engaging in risky behavior and promotes youth acting in productive ways. The data consistently show that the power of assets is cumulative: the more assets young people experience, the more apt they are to succeed in school and live positive lives, and the less likely they are to participate in high-risk behaviors such as drug use, violence, and early sexual activity.

Most of this book is built around helping students develop the "internal" Developmental Assets of values, skills, and self-perceptions contained in the Positive Values and Social Competencies asset categories, and, to a lesser extent, in the Positive Identity category. But each of the eight asset categories relates in broad terms to the values and choices involved in sexuality and sex education.

Parents, teachers, and other adults need to give **support** in the form of love and encouragement to all young people. All young people have questions about sex, and the great majority will have sexual experiences before marriage. Their questions deserve to be answered. And what if your student thinks she might be a lesbian, or he might be gay, or what if she has never felt like a girl and feels in her core that she is a he? If you listen with understanding and caring, you are truly being supportive by accepting your students for who they are, and showing other young people in your classroom how to do the same.

The **empowerment** assets are about students feeling safe, useful, and listened to. Providing a class environment that doesn't allow sexist or homophobic comments helps kids feel emotionally safe. And helping students understand sexual harassment, identify signs of possibly dangerous dating situations that could lead to rape, and discuss other forms of sexual aggression helps keep them physically safe, too. Asking for students' opinions about sex-related topics (once they have demonstrated through their assignments that they know what the facts are) gives students the message that their voices are valuable. Even community service activities—another part of empowerment—can be set up to help students learn about sexuality.

Parents set the primary **boundaries and expectations**—family values about when having sex is acceptable and when it isn't—but educators play a big role in urging young people to delay sexual activity as long as possible because they equip students with facts that help them understand that waiting to have sex is generally better for their physical and emotional well-being. Expecting students to be well informed about sex-related topics before they share their opinions is a key expectation, too. Many people have emotional feelings about such sexuality-related topics as homosexuality, or how effective condoms are in preventing HIV. Students are allowed to have their feelings and values, but they must also be expected to know what the facts are. Where sex is concerned, the facts are often very much at odds with what people believe to be true. And setting guidelines for having a nonsexist, nonhomophobic class environment of honest, fact-based discussion about sex sets a tone of expectation that everyone is to be respected, and medical accuracy and scientific honesty are the foundation of informed opinions and debate.

Kids who are supported in **constructive use of their time** and are involved in high-quality after-school programs generally do better in school and do a better job of avoiding risky behaviors such as early or unprotected sex and substance use. Individual teachers can lobby their administrators to make sure there are plenty of after-school program options for students. Schools do their part to foster healthier sex-related decisions, as well as other kinds of positive behavior, by making sure that co-curricular programs are plentiful and well staffed.

The main focus of this book is on the internal assets. Activities and discussions encourage students to explore how they feel about their **positive values**—where they stand with regard to issues of equality and justice, honesty, integrity, responsibility, and personal restraint.

Students will also experience activities that give them a chance to practice their **social competencies**. They'll try out communication strategies and discover ways to get their feelings across to other people. They'll work on their decision-making skills and practice their resistance skills. They'll also have the chance to explore how they feel about themselves and develop a sense of **positive identity** that will give them the strength of character to make decisions that they know are right for them, and to communicate those decisions to others.

And finally, a **commitment to learning** is also relevant: science and public policy and laws around sex-related issues change often. New contraceptive methods are developed and new laws passed that affect what we know and what is or is not culturally accepted. In order to live as sexually healthy and responsible as possible, students (and their teachers!) need to always be aware of new knowledge, laws, and policies. Whether it is about teens' access to contraceptives, the transmissibility of various sexually transmitted infections, the facts about sexual orientation or gender identity, parental notification of abortions, or the issue of marriage equality, science and the law on sex-related topics rarely stand still. So, a commitment to lifelong learning is a very important sex education asset—possibly the most important sex education asset—to have.

The Framework of 40 Developmental Assets® for Adolescents

Search Institute has identified the following building blocks of healthy development that help young people grow up healthy, caring, and responsible. This framework will be used as a reference point throughout the book.

EXTERNAL ASSETS

Support

1. **Family Support**—Family life provides high levels of love and support.
2. **Positive Family Communication**—Young person and her or his parent(s) communicate positively, and young person is willing to seek advice and counsel from parent(s).
3. **Other Adult Relationships**—Young person receives support from three or more non-parent adults.
4. **Caring Neighborhood**—Young person experiences caring neighbors.
5. **Caring School Climate**—School provides a caring, encouraging environment.
6. **Parent Involvement in Schooling**—Parent(s) are actively involved in helping young person succeed in school.

Empowerment

7. **Community Values Youth**—Young person perceives that adults in the community value youth.
8. **Youth as Resources**—Young people are given useful roles in the community.
9. **Service to Others**—Young person serves in the community one hour or more per week.
10. **Safety**—Young person feels safe at home, at school, and in the neighborhood.

Boundaries and Expectations

11. **Family Boundaries**—Family has clear rules and consequences and monitors the young person's whereabouts.
12. **School Boundaries**—School provides clear rules and consequences.
13. **Neighborhood Boundaries**—Neighbors take responsibility for monitoring young people's behavior.
14. **Adult Role Models**—Parent(s) and other adults model positive, responsible behavior.
15. **Positive Peer Influence**—Young person's best friends model responsible behavior.
16. **High Expectations**—Both parent(s) and teachers encourage the young person to do well.

Constructive Use of Time

17. **Creative Activities**—Young person spends three or more hours per week in lessons or practice in music, theater, or other arts.
18. **Youth Programs**—Young person spends three or more hours per week in sports, clubs, or organizations at school and/or in the community.
19. **Religious Community**—Young person spends one or more hours per week in activities in a religious institution.
20. **Time at Home**—Young person is out with friends "with nothing special to do" two or fewer nights per week.

INTERNAL ASSETS

Commitment to Learning

21. **Achievement Motivation**—Young person is motivated to do well in school.
22. **School Engagement**—Young person is actively engaged in learning.
23. **Homework**—Young person reports doing at least one hour of homework every school day.
24. **Bonding to School**—Young person cares about her or his school.
25. **Reading for Pleasure**—Young person reads for pleasure three or more hours per week.

Positive Values

26. **Caring**—Young person places high value on helping other people.
27. **Equality and Social Justice**—Young person places high value on promoting equality and reducing hunger and poverty.
28. **Integrity**—Young person acts on convictions and stands up for her or his beliefs.
29. **Honesty**—Young person "tells the truth even when it is not easy."
30. **Responsibility**—Young person accepts and takes personal responsibility.
31. **Restraint**—Young person believes it is important not to be sexually active or to use alcohol or other drugs.

Social Competencies

32. **Planning and Decision Making**—Young person knows how to plan ahead and make choices.
33. **Interpersonal Competence**—Young person has empathy, sensitivity, and friendship skills.
34. **Cultural Competence**—Young person has knowledge of and comfort with people of different cultural/racial/ethnic backgrounds.
35. **Resistance Skills**—Young person can resist negative peer pressure and dangerous situations.
36. **Peaceful Conflict Resolution**—Young person seeks to resolve conflict nonviolently.

Positive Identity

37. **Personal Power**—Young person feels he or she has control over "things that happen to me."
38. **Self-Esteem**—Young person reports having a high self-esteem.
39. **Sense of Purpose**—Young person reports that "my life has a purpose."
40. **Positive View of Personal Future**—Young person is optimistic about her or his personal future.

This handout may be reproduced for educational, noncommercial uses only (with this copyright line). From *Healthy Teen Relationships: Using Values and Choices to Teach Sex Education* by Martha R. Roper. Copyright © 2011 by Search Institute®, Minneapolis, Minnesota, 877-240-7251 ext. 1, www.search-institute.org. All rights reserved.

Acknowledgments

This book comes at the end of a 40-year career in teaching, so to thank everyone by name is impossible. However, there were groups, and a few individuals, who nurtured me throughout the decades.

My editors, Kate Brielmaier and Karl Anderson, worked diligently on my manuscript. It's hard to talk about the right way to discuss sexuality for an often shy and extremely polite audience. Kate and Karl wanted me to be open about what I have done in the classroom to help other health and sex education teachers give kids the information and skills they need to know to have good values and make good choices.

Michael Carerra, Helen Manley, Ronald Flowers, and Sol Gordon all trained or influenced me in the '70s.

Doug Kirby, Pam Wilson, Konnie McCaffree, and Mary Lee Tatum were among the first mentors and friends who were dedicated to me as we marched through the decades together.

In the '80s a group we named ASET—Advanced Sexuality Educators and Trainers—banded together for support, and this group has lasted 25 years. The group members continue to encourage me, inform me, and challenge me.

Two public school districts invited me to teach health and sex education at the high school level—The School District of University City, Missouri, and Parkway School District, Chesterfield, Missouri. Both Boards of Education were courageous at times in supporting me and sex education. I want to thank all of my superintendents and principals who worked with me and worried with me throughout the decades of challenges.

Teachers in every decade have mentored me and supported me on a daily basis. They knew me, and they trusted me.

My family has been more than patient and supportive about my writing for the last year. My husband, Peter C. Scales, has been my primary inspiration and support since his first book about the opposition to sex education in the '70s. The love and friendship we have transcends the battles we have fought together.

To all these, my deepest thanks.

Finally, I am dedicating this book to all of my students and their families. My work, influenced by all of those groups and people listed above, lives on through them.

Introduction

A full-time health teacher in public schools since 1974, I wrote this book to help others who want to teach a sex education class in a school, a religious youth group, or any other community group because they want kids to have a place to learn about and discuss sexuality and values in a group setting with an informed, trained adult. A valued friend and sexuality educator, Mary Lee Tatum, once said, "Our culture treats sex as pornographic. The classroom is one of the few places where kids can safely and sanely talk about sex, including how to say no." All of us who value sexuality as a natural function and expression of our humanity also want our children to grow up with a healthy and positive attitude about sexuality, with medically accurate information and values that emphasize our shared sense of personal dignity and shared respect toward this sensitive subject simply called "sex."

The lessons in this book can be integrated into a health class, or they can be used as a stand-alone course outside the school. Search Institute, the originator of the *Human Sexuality: Values & Choices* program, first published that values-based curriculum for seventh and eighth grades in the 1980s. The evaluation of the program was positive in terms of increasing knowledge and enhancing students' values when making sexual decisions. However, after a 1991 revision, the *Values & Choices* program was left on the shelf for twenty years. This book is not intended to replace the original *Values & Choices*, but it is intended to take the Search Institute Developmental Assets approach to sex education and combine it with the latest research on what works in preventing teen pregnancy, sexually transmitted infections and diseases, and to give the teacher a short and user-friendly manual that will, in one book, make a positive impact on the students' values and choices about their sexuality.

Without education about sexuality, our young people are deprived of an area of their schooling that can provide them with the knowledge, values, and skills that will carry them into their adulthood and into their own parenting experience. Most people choose to get married, and most choose to have children, so why would we deny them information about how to make the most important decisions of their lives? Kids need to hear what their parents believe about sexual decisions and to learn the facts about their bodies and their sexuality. Even if the only thing we agree on is that sex education is part of our education about our health and wellness, we are on the right track for future generations.

Additionally, sex education is not just for the student—it is for the families students will produce and teach to live as sexually healthy and caring adults. One of my former students, now a parent of school-age children, told me that my sex education class twenty years ago prepared him for so many of the little talks that led to the "big talk." When his daughter was five, she said: "Daddy, I now know the difference between boys and girls. Girls have feelings." My student said he laughed out loud, and was not only able to jump right into talking about feelings that all people have, but was also able to cover other similarities and differences without feeling uncomfortable.

I have stayed with teaching in high schools because in those classrooms a teacher can create caring, ongoing relationships. In school or small groups anywhere, a teacher can emphasize how to find medically accurate information and help kids identify their values and make good choices based on thoughtful consideration of the facts. Yes, people may disagree even when they work from the same set of facts, but in school they learn and practice how to disagree in a civil way.

A Philosophy of Sex Education

When it comes to the issues to emphasize in a sex education program, I have chosen to write lessons that can be integrated into a school health course requirement. Comprehensive sex education, which teaches and promotes abstinence but also includes lessons on pregnancy and disease prevention, has been evaluated and found effective if certain criteria are faithfully executed.

That said, reducing teen pregnancy, birth, and the rate of sexually transmitted infections (STIs) is not enough for most of us when it comes to educating our youth about sexuality. There is so much more to teach that we feel certain will help guide them through the potentially rough and hopefully joyful waters of adolescence.

Our culture is still split over whether talking about sex is a good thing. Research does not seem able to nail down the positive effects of talking with students about values and attitudes toward sexuality. But it seems to be common sense that we should be open to listening to kids talk about their concerns and questions. If we cannot prove that talking about sexual values in relationships improves sexual relationships, should we stop talking about them with kids? No. Not only should parents and trusted adults listen and talk with kids, teachers from all disciplines should take advantage of teachable moments.

This week a girl who was wearing a T-shirt that said "Blink if you think I'm hot" told me that I needed to be careful online. Trying *not* to blink, I asked with concern: "What do I need to be careful about?" She said that if I started video-chatting I might meet an "old creeper dude" trying to pick me up. "How old *are* these men who are going to try to pick me up?" I asked with pseudo-naiveté. "They *could* be forty years old!" she replied. It took the students a couple of seconds for it to sink in that I am in my 60s, and we all started laughing at once. There were so many directions in which to take that teachable moment that it was hard to know where to start. We spent about 30 minutes unpacking that suitcase and looking at all the issues the girl raised—including her choice of T-shirts. I ended it by telling the class that I was writing a book for teachers on how to teach sex education and then asking them to write down what they think other kids want to know about sex.

If it's your first time teaching sex education, you might be surprised by the range of questions students ask. But the questions on most of those 3" x 5" cards are similar to the questions my students asked in the '70s, '80s, '90s, and all the way to the present:

1. Why is sex the main topic on our minds?
2. What is the right age to have sex?
3. Is sex bad?
4. Does masturbation stunt your growth?
5. How can you have sex and not get pregnant or get a disease?
6. *How* do people have sex?
7. Tell us about birth control and abortion.
8. What is pornography?

Newer questions—but not completely new—are about oral sex, anal sex, the morning-after pill, and why people question other people's sexuality. Some questions, of course, were personal to me about my sexual experience and whether I thought girls would like to get "gang banged." "It's not polite to ask anyone about their sexual experience—even your parents," I told them as I briefly went over some of their questions and answered the easy ones. "And about wanting to get raped? You know the answer to that—except the way the question was phrased made it seem like a male sexual fantasy."

You will have to decide for yourself what you want to teach and how much you let the students pull out of you what they really want to know. If you are new to the field, stick to the curriculum that is approved. If you are not new to the field, stick to the curriculum that is approved, *and* be sensitively responsive to the students who let you know what is really on their minds. You can, with humor and respect for all religions and diversity of humankind, do both.

How do you know when you can give more information? When you have experienced support from your supervisor for answering this type of question or concern before and a parent complained to the same supervisor you have now, I would consider it safe to be more open about your answer. If you have no experience with your new principal, have a chat before you teach your sex ed unit and let her know what kinds of phone calls might come and how her predecessor handled it in the past. Ask if you have her support and observe her body language. My principal tells parents whether it's a rumor or whether it is an experienced teacher's answer. He tells parents what I probably said in response to the student's question, and then he verifies that with me. For example, if parents have heard about my lesson that includes descriptions of offensive writing on T-shirts, they may have heard different versions than I described. The T-shirt that says, "My Wiener Does Tricks" and shows a stick-figure boy and a stick-figure dog always brings a laugh because it's edgy. It's not dirty, and it is funny, but that does not make it appropriate to wear to school. Our school dress code states clearly that there should not be sexual innuendoes on clothing.

About This Book

This book is intended for teachers who want to promote a positive approach, using values and choices as a takeoff point in their sex education unit. Others may want to add a lesson or two into their health, social studies, communication arts, family and consumer science, or community youth group curriculum. These lessons promote healthy teen relationships and positive sexuality: the things we practitioners teach because we see the effect of our work—even when research cannot prove it "works." Some of the lessons at the end are proven to help prevent pregnancy and HIV infection as shown from the research of Douglas Kirby: saying no, using birth control, and using condoms.[1] Only *you* know what you'll be able to use from this book after you have read it.

Chapter 1 discusses common characteristics of effective sex education, while chapter 2 gives instructors a firm foundation in how to teach it, providing tips and lessons learned from my experience of 37 years as a public school classroom teacher of health and sexuality. Chapter 3 features activities that help you introduce the topic of sex ed and set up ground rules for students to follow, emphasizing thoughtful discussion and a willingness to listen.

Chapter 4 provides lessons that take sex ed from an abstract topic to a practical reality, allowing students to explore how they would react to the implications of sexuality and the consequences of sex in the "real world." And chapter 5 features lessons that encourage teens to have open and honest discussions about sex with their partners and with their parents or other trusted adults.

You'll also see sidebars labeled "Real Thoughts from Teens." Chapter 3 begins with an exercise called "The Question Box" that asks teens to write their questions and comments about sex on index cards and drop them in a box. I do this with my students each semester, and some of the cards I've received over the years are featured in these sidebars. Some questions and comments are thoughtful, some unexpected, and some uncomfortable, but all are real examples of what teens want to know about sex.

This book is by no means complete in terms of what an adolescent needs to know, but combined with the Developmental Assets approach to youth development and other resources found online or from other books on your shelf, you will be able to give your students and their families more than you ever thought you could.

I hope that the wisdom imparted and the lessons and resources shared here will make you as comfortable as you can possibly be as you incorporate these lessons into your curriculum. Pick and choose to add to the enduring understandings and essential questions of your program or school mission.

Guiding Principles for Sex Educators

- Sex education is different from other classes.
- Your supervisors, your students' parents, and your board members must approve your program.

- Get to know the people you work for, and let them know that you are a good person who is qualified to teach this unique subject.
- You must be trained in teaching sexuality education before you teach it.
- Every student gets the same information.
- Be careful about people who claim to be guest speakers in one area but who are actually trying to find a way to talk with young people about their hidden agendas.
- There are no electronics allowed in class: no text messages, no email messages, no Internet surfing, no video recording.
- Do not be Facebook friends (or use other online social networks) with students.
- Keep your evaluators and superiors aware of potential problems as they come up.
- Ask students, counselors, evaluators, and anyone associated with your program to let you know if you are being talked about.
- Network constantly to promote sex education, but do not debate people whom you know will twist what you say.
- Be careful when ordering sex education materials and supplies with taxpayer funds.
- Try to help students understand that sexuality should be a positive part of our lives, *and* that it is so powerful an influence that we have to be careful that our sexual choices as teenagers do not have adult consequences. It's hard to keep saying that in a way that feels positive, but we have to keep trying. People do better with a health challenge than a health threat.
- Everyone deserves to feel lovable and capable and normal.
- Adolescents need to feel that they get to hold their personal opinions, even when their opinions are not based on fact.
- Students learn from each other through discussion.
- Students learn about who the teacher really is when she or he is arguing with another student about anything—being late for class, tone of voice, throwing a wad of paper, or talking in class. Therefore, it is essential that teachers be excellent role models of communication and conflict management skills.
- Do not draw a penis or vulva so artistically that students think of it as pornography.
- It's okay to tell the class that you feel embarrassed about something.
- It's okay to have a sense of humor.
- It's okay to share your opinion as long as you tell the students it is your opinion and touch your hat that says "Teacher's Opinion" (see page 27).

Endnote

1. Kirby, Douglas, "Emerging Answers: New Research Findings on Programs to Reduce Teen Pregnancy." Washington, DC: National Campaign to Prevent Teen and Unplanned Pregnancy, 2007.

Chapter 1

Characteristics of Effective Sex Education

In spite of the good news in recent decades about teenagers and sexuality, there is bad news: many teenagers still grow up ignorant about sexuality and therefore become victims to the people who try to prey on them. Of all abused or maltreated children in the United States, less than 10 percent experience sexual abuse (and sexual abuse as a whole has declined more than 50 percent since 1992), but the need to educate kids about potential abuse is still critical.[1] Sexually transmitted infections and AIDS are a continuing worry. While some parents want sex education to scare their children out of sex, the scare technique doesn't work. As human beings, we are naturally curious about our sexuality, and we will have sexual feelings and experiences, with or without education.

In a sexualized society such as ours, parents should be the first sex educators, and the school should support parents and give even more age-appropriate lessons in an organized group setting where students can learn from a trained teacher

REAL THOUGHTS FROM TEENS

"A lot of people talk about sex these days. I mean cartoons even talk about sex! My cousin is in the fifth grade and he knows about porn."

who can facilitate important discussions. We want to be positive about sexuality and to tell kids about the pleasure and joy it adds to our lives, and yet we want them to understand its power and potential to harm us if managed badly. Many sex educators, counselors, and therapists, along with parents of school-age children, fear that there is so much emphasis on prevention of bad things that can happen as a result of sexual activity that we forget to emphasize the lifelong pleasure, comfort, joy, and stability it should bring to our lives.

That said, information about sexuality is not enough. We can teach students to communicate and manage the conflict that naturally occurs in relationships. Even basic communication skills are bound to increase the quality and longevity of those relationships. We can promote the internal assets of positive values, and we can promote social competencies in our lessons, but how do we know that sex education "works"? What does it mean for sex education to "work"?

In a report called "Emerging Answers: Research Findings on Programs to Reduce Teen Pregnancy and Sexually Transmitted Diseases" Douglas Kirby states that:

for decades, dedicated adults have worked with teens to prevent unintended pregnancy. Their efforts have been rewarded with declining rates of pregnancy and childbirth.

Prevention efforts have also resulted in lower rates of some STDs. An increasingly robust body of research is clarifying the types of behavior that most strongly affect pregnancy and STD/HIV transmission, is identifying the factors that influence sexual risk-taking and is revealing the effects of programs on teen sexual behavior and rates of pregnancy and STD. Yet pregnancy and STD rates are still high, and both more research and more effective programs are needed.[2]

Dr. Kirby says that when communities plan a program, they must plan it based on what has shown success in other courses. For example, such programs must be straightforward and specific. They might discuss realistic situations that could lead to unprotected sex and methods for avoiding those situations, for remaining abstinent, and for using condoms and other contraceptives.

REAL THOUGHTS FROM TEENS

"What's the average size of a penis?"

Overall, about two-thirds of the curriculum-based sex and STI/HIV education programs studied have had positive effects on teen sexual behavior. For example, they delayed the initiation of sex, increased condom or contraceptive use, or both. Virtually all of the programs also improved sexual protective factors. The programs had mixed, but encouraging, effects on reducing teen pregnancy, childbearing, and STIs.

Characteristics of Effective Curriculum-Based Programs

The process of developing the curriculum

1. Involves multiple people with expertise in theory, research, and sex and STI/HIV education to develop the curriculum
2. Assesses relevant needs and assets of the target group
3. Uses a logic model approach that specifies the health goals, the types of behavior affecting those goals, the risk and protective factors affecting those types of behavior, and activities to change those risk and protective factors
4. Designs activities consistent with community values and available resources (e.g., staff time, staff skills, facility space and supplies)
5. Pilot-tests the program

The contents of the curriculum itself

6. Focus on clear health goals—the prevention of STI/HIV, pregnancy, or both
7. Focus narrowly on specific types of behavior leading to these health goals (e.g., abstaining from sex or using condoms or other contraceptives), give clear messages about these types of behavior, and address situations that might lead to them and how to avoid them
8. Address sexual psychosocial risk and protective factors that affect sexual behavior (e.g., knowledge, perceived risks, values, attitudes, perceived norms, and self-efficacy) and change them using activities and teaching methodologies

9. Creates a safe social environment for young people to participate
10. Includes multiple activities to change each of the targeted risk and protective factors
11. Employs instructionally sound teaching methods that actively involve participants, that help them personalize the information, and that are designed to change the targeted risk and protective factors
12. Employs activities, instructional methods, and behavioral messages that are appropriate to the teens' culture, developmental age, and sexual experience
13. Covers topics in a logical sequence
14. Secures at least minimal support from appropriate authorities, such as departments of health, school districts, or community organizations
15. Selects educators with desired characteristics (whenever possible), trains them, and provides monitoring, supervision, and support
16. If needed, implements activities to recruit and retain teens and overcome barriers to their involvement (e.g., publicizes the program, offers food, or obtains consent)
17. Implements virtually all activities with reasonable fidelity[3]

Dr. Kirby also notes that in addition to these characteristics of effective curricula, effective programs also provided training for the educators and on implementing the program. In general, the training was designed to give teachers information on the program as well as practice using the teaching strategies included in the curriculum.[4]

Unfortunately, there are no "magic bullets" that completely eliminate unprotected intercourse among adolescents, but when teachers are trained and faithful to the curriculum, it is more likely that students' behavior and values will change for the better.

It is my hope that people who work with kids in the area of sex education will pay attention to the changes in society that require us to be vigilant in our efforts to raise healthy kids. We must connect the dots between the research about effective sex education and the research of Search Institute about how positive values can help kids make wise personal choices relating to their sexuality.

Shared Guidelines for Sex Education

In 1991, I was invited to be a participant on the Sex Information and Education Council of the United States (SIECUS) task force, which released the Guidelines for Comprehensive Sexuality Education: Kindergarten–12th Grade. The Guidelines represented the first national model for comprehensive sexuality education and helped educators evaluate existing curricula and create new programs. The Guidelines are based on a number of values about sexuality, young people, and the role of families. While these values reflect those of many communities across the country, they are not universal. Parents, educators, and community members will need to review these values to be sure that the program that is implemented is consistent with their community's beliefs, culture, and social norms.

The values inherent in the Guidelines are:

- Every person has dignity and self-worth.
- All children should be loved and cared for.
- Young people should view themselves as unique and worthwhile individuals within the context of their cultural heritage.
- Sexuality is a natural and healthy part of living.
- All persons are sexual.
- Sexuality includes physical, ethical, social, spiritual, psychological, and emotional dimensions.
- Individuals can express their sexuality in varied ways.
- Parents should be the primary sexuality educators of their children.
- Families should provide children's first education about sexuality.
- Families should share their values about sexuality with their children.
- In a pluralistic society, people should respect and accept the diversity of values and beliefs about sexuality that exist in a community.
- Sexual relationships should be reciprocal, based on respect, and should never be coercive or exploitative.
- All persons have the right and obligation to make responsible sexual choices.
- Individuals, families, and society benefit when children are able to discuss sexuality with their parents and/or trusted adults.
- Young people develop their values about sexuality as part of becoming adults.
- Young people explore their sexuality as a natural process in achieving sexual maturity.
- Early involvement in sexual behaviors poses risks.
- Abstaining from sexual intercourse is the most effective method of preventing pregnancy and STI/HIV.
- Young people who are involved in sexual relationships need access to information about healthcare services.[5]

Working inside public schools for 40 years, I have seen several generations of not only students, but also waves of school reform. The first year I taught, 1970, in

REAL THOUGHTS FROM TEENS
"How do you say no?"

Washington, D.C., Public Schools, the teachers were told that if we did not raise every child's reading to grade-level expectation by the end of the school year we would not be rehired. Without naming the school reform trends that came and went during these last decades, I will say that teachers are constantly revising their lesson plans to meet local, state, and national guidelines. Frankly, I enjoy it. It helps me step back and see with new eyes what we wrote and make improvements.

While there is conflict and endless discussion about whether teachers should all be teaching from the same page and testing on the same chapter on a given day, I find that complying quickly and graciously is in the best interests of the students and your working relationships inside your organization. Save your energy for battles you can win.

The Centers for Disease Control's School Health Education Resources: National Health Education Standards (NHES)[6]

Standard 1: Students will comprehend concepts related to health promotion and disease prevention to enhance health.

Standard 2: Students will analyze the influence of family, peers, culture, media, technology, and other factors on health behaviors.

Standard 3: Students will demonstrate the ability to access valid information, products, and services to enhance health.

Standard 4: Students will demonstrate the ability to use interpersonal communication skills to enhance health and avoid or reduce health risks.

Standard 5: Students will demonstrate the ability to use decision-making skills to enhance health.

Standard 6: Students will demonstrate the ability to use goal-setting skills to enhance health.

Standard 7: Students will demonstrate the ability to practice health-enhancing behaviors and avoid or reduce health risks.

Standard 8: Students will demonstrate the ability to advocate for personal, family, and community health.

You will also need to know what your state's Department of Education standards are. I found these by calling my health coordinator in my school district. He referred me to the Missouri Department of Education health coordinator, who sent me to the website of the Missouri state standards (dese.mo.gov/standards/healthed.html). The Missouri standards are fairly typical of state standards:

In Health/Physical Education, students in Missouri public schools will acquire a solid foundation which includes knowledge of

1. structures of, functions of, and relationships among human body systems
2. principles and practices of physical and mental health (such as personal health habits, nutrition, stress management)
3. diseases and methods for prevention, treatment and control
4. principles of movement and physical fitness

5. methods used to assess health, reduce risk factors, and avoid high risk behaviors (such as violence, tobacco, alcohol and other drug use)

6. consumer health issues (such as the effects of mass media and technologies on safety and health)

7. responses to emergency situations

Talking about Sex, Politics, and Religion

The United States Supreme Court hands down rulings having to do with education and religion, so we as teachers should pay attention to the cases that have an effect on our teaching. We also need to become familiar with our own contract for teaching and what is written there to guide us about what to say when we try to combine the three topics some people feel we are not supposed to talk about: sex, politics, and religion.

When I left University City School District, in University City, Missouri, after thirteen years of teaching a high school course called Human Sexuality, I was given a plaque that commended me for bringing "Credit not Controversy" to our community. Sex education is inherently controversial, and if truth be told, even in that supportive environment there were complaints about my course. The principals did have to come and talk with me and gather information about what had happened from my perspective. I made mistakes (that I was careful not to repeat). Usually those mistakes were about stepping on the toes of people who felt that I did not respect their religion. Now that religion is more involved than ever in politics and sexuality, it is even more important to be confident about how to talk about the America we live in today.

> State statutes also guide our school board policies. The state statutes can be more important than the federal guidelines because some people run for the state legislature on one platform: against sex education. Knowing the laws and the policies of the state may help avoid some problems. At the beginning of the sex education unit, I stand in front of the class and read the students the ten requirements for sex education from my state's (Missouri) state legislature. Why invite trouble?

REAL THOUGHTS FROM TEENS

"Why is it that having sex makes a guy a player, which is a good thing, but it makes [a girl] a slut and a ho?"

Learn about religion—and not just your own, but all the major world religions. Pay attention to what is going on in the country that blends sex, politics, and religion, and what your students will be hearing about at home and talking about in class. Protect each student's right to have their religion or lack of religion respected at school. If you are not a member of a faith community, that is your right. Many people are not. That said, I like to be a member of a local church. Holding my "opinion hat" (see page 27), I tell students that I am religious so they can see that I can talk about sex and still be a religious (i.e., "good") person. You can remind students that all major religions have overt or subtle teachings about sexuality, and encourage them to talk with their parents and their own religious clergy about the concerns they have.

"Best Practices" for Sex Education

I have a few tips on how to make your teaching look effortless while you walk the tight-rope above a crowd of attentive and nervous parents, colleagues, school board members, religious groups, and neighbors.

1. **Live in the community where you teach.** There is nothing like being a taxpayer in your own school community. That way, your own partner can appear before the Board of Education during the public comments. You can talk in your neighborhood about what a great school district you work in. That's your story. Stick to it. Remember that everything you say about people will get back to them—even the good things. You can join committees made up of citizens and wear two or three hats—taxpayer, employee, and parent. However, you might be a graduate of the program or high school where you teach. It may be impossible to afford to live in the community where you teach. In that case, it is even more important to develop multiple networks for support. Find out who among the supportive agencies does have employees who live in your school district, and ask them to help you when you need it. You are allowed to work to elect board members even if you do not live in the district. You can recruit supportive parents to join health advisory committees. Many decisions are made by stakeholders long before they come to a public committee vote, so make sure you stay aware of what is going on.

2. **Become a known stakeholder in how your school district is run.** Get involved not only in the sex education program, but also the health program and curriculum as well as the vision and mission of the school district. Join community projects and go to the meetings so you are known as the nice person you are. People are less likely to believe a rumor about you if they have met you.

3. **Promote sex education in the public square.** There are many ways to do this: organize teacher workshops, ask to be interviewed on radio and television, write a letter to the editor or a commentary piece for the newspaper, join organizations, and do local and national work with advocacy projects.

4. **Work to elect school board members who believe in comprehensive health education** and are not likely to be afraid of residents who stand up to blast sex education during the public comment sessions before board meetings.

5. **Keep your administrators and your evaluators aware of your curriculum and invite them to come and see you teach.** Let them experience your style. Invite them to talk with you about rumors they hear so you can become a part of the solution instead of the problem. I admit that sometimes my style is the problem. I have a sense of humor, and I sometimes provide more information than students are used to hearing from a teacher. When a parent complained about this, the

principal asked her if she would complain about her son getting too much information about calculus.

6. **Always be a model of good citizenship in the neighborhood and community where you live.** There is no such thing as getting away from who you are. Expect to meet people who live in your school district even when you're halfway around the world. Be a good, responsible, law-abiding citizen who really does live up to the highest ideals of this country. Live to leave a legacy that will make your family proud.

7. **Learn how to take criticism and argue your points fairly.** You cannot have everything you want at work. Carefully pick what you do want and give up the rest graciously and quickly, and don't go looking for a fight. However, if someone starts a fight with you over politics and religion, then you will have to stand up for yourself. Hopefully, you will be able to resolve the conflict in any number of ways that are agreeable to your principal and the parents. If the person who picks a fight with you is a student, you have many more opportunities to listen to that student's views and let her share those views with the class.

8. **Do not engage in dead-end battles with parents who will never agree with you.** Ask what they want from you regarding their own child's experience in your class. I tell parents they can have one of two results: either I can change something for that child during that course, or I can change the offending piece of the class for students in the future. Find out what they want and see if you can give it to them. When the "offending" piece is part of the state-mandated curriculum, there is nothing to offer but perhaps a change of style in your own presentation.

9. **Allow students to be taken out of your sex education class for any part that a parent or student might feel uncomfortable with.** Granted, sex education is not comfortable for most students at some point, and that is normal. However, for parents who are extremely concerned, arrangements can be made for the student to leave during certain lessons with no grades or feelings hurt. Other students do not have to know.

10. **Tell parents: "What you say to your children is much more important than what one high school health teacher said one day in a semester-long class."** I tell them that the important thing is to use my class as a jumping-off point to explain what they believe about any topic. I tell them that they can say: "I don't care what Ms. Roper said! Here's what I believe!" This usually gets a laugh.

11. **Try to stay up to date on what is happening in the legislative, judicial, and executive branches of the government.** It is important for students to know how their country works. At home, students may be locked into one way of thinking and viewing the world, but educators in all disciplines, and especially in sex education, find it valuable to talk about and follow many issues while the course is in session.

12. **Have an "opinion hat"—or anything else that signals you're sharing your opinion on a topic.** I use a large hat with a wide band, and tucked into the band is a 4" x 6" index card with "Ms. Roper's opinion" written on it. I tell students that most of what I say in class is not my opinion, but when it is, I will walk over to my hat and put it on while I talk. People do worry that teachers have more influence over children this age than their parents or clergy do. Maybe that is true, but it shouldn't stop us from having a conversation about what we believe and why.

Working Through Conflict

My experience is that most conflicts with parents come not directly from the parents themselves, but through the principal. Since our topic is sex related, it is charged with emotion—usually embarrassment and anger. Some of my colleagues around the country have been invited to talk with the local school board about their programs only to get there and see hundreds of people eager to yell at them.

I never like seeing my principals at my door. I never like seeing an e-mail from my evaluator. My stomach still gets that sinking feeling every time I listen to what they have to say. I am lucky to be married to a psychologist (who always happens to be *in* and will always see me on short notice), and my son is a lawyer. I also have my own lawyer, who has donated hours of his time over my long career because he believes in what I'm teaching. But when I was young I couldn't afford the kind of counseling and attorneys' fees that I needed. My teachers' association was and has been helpful, and so have my network of personal friends and colleagues around the country who are also sex educators. Our support group has grown from 20 people to 150 people, and we communicate online every day. I suggest cultivating your own sources of support, especially by reaching out to other sexuality educators.

The amount of time I've spent working out problems is really very small considering that I've been teaching sex education in a public school since 1974. Here are the basics of how to hear a complaint and what to do:

> **REAL THOUGHTS FROM TEENS**
>
> **"Why do people talk about sex all the time? How do you stop thinking/talking about it?"**

1. **Listen carefully to every word and evaluate whether this is a serious complaint.**
   Is this coming directly from a student, another teacher, a parent, a principal, or someone else? If it feels serious, it may be, but most complaints I've had did not turn out to be serious. Embarrassing, yes, but not serious. Listening carefully and asking questions works if it is a private conversation. Most people want problems to go away, and they are willing to work it out quickly. Everyone feels better, and then we all go on with our lives. However, there are people who thrive on conflict, and they are worthy of your concern, because if you make a mistake with them, you may become their project for the next few months.

2. **Do not resign.** Do not sign anything. Do not admit guilt or accept blame until you know what you are accused of.

3. **Develop and maintain good relationships with your principals.** They are the ones who will probably get the call.

4. **Do not make any public statements.**

5. **Write everything down from the beginning of what happened.** Continue to keep accurate notes with dates. Devote a notebook to this topic and print every e-mail and note about it, and keep the notes in chronological order.

6. **Request and keep all documents relating to the complaint.**

7. **Assume that everything we say and do will appear on the Internet.** Stay calm and courteous. Ask clarifying questions.

8. **Ask someone to go with you when attending a meeting with the parent or the principal.** You have a right to have someone with you, and if a topic comes up that involves private information about a student, then you can take that item off the agenda for that meeting. You do not have to be alone in meetings where people are yelling at you.

9. **Call for help if you feel that you are being threatened and that you are in danger.** If you are in immediate physical danger, try to leave the area and call 911. If you need to call your principal or your teachers' association representative, then do it. You are allowed to get up and leave the room when you feel uncomfortable. Go to an administrator's office and ask that person to go to the parents in your room. Call the police if you receive a death threat, or call the FBI if the threat is from a person in another state.

Write a Letter to Parents

Always write a letter to parents introducing yourself and telling them about the sex ed class their teenager will be taking. Note that they do not need to contact you or return this form unless they do *not* want their son or daughter to be in your class. Invite them to call to see if there is one particular lesson or part of a lesson they do not want their teen to hear. Since the Board of Education created a pull-out policy starting in 1992, I have had only two students leave the classroom for the whole unit (their parents were followers of a religious faith that specifically forbade unmarried people from learning about sexuality). Another girl's mom asked that her daughter be allowed to leave class whenever she felt uncomfortable, which was once. So out of the last 6,000 students, only three parents have had a problem with the sexuality part of my class.

My principal feels it is important for him to receive a copy of this letter for his files in case a parent calls. A sample letter is below, to help you get started. Also below is a handout for parents and guardians that you may want to include with the letter. It provides parents and guardians with tips for conducting a productive and useful conversation with teachers about sexuality.

Dear Parents of Ms. Roper's Health Classes,

It is the end of the semester, and it's time to teach about Disease Prevention and Healthful Relationships. The subjects come up often, but I have been postponing certain lessons so you can have your son or daughter removed from class if you choose to do so.

I will show the PG-13 rated video *Juno* on May 14 and May 15. I will lead a discussion about decision making, and I will promote abstinence as the only 100 percent effective method of pregnancy prevention. I will show a video about contraception on May 18 and May 19.

We have studied sexually transmitted diseases and HIV/AIDS already, but I will show the Parkway-produced two-minute video on disease prevention on May 18 and May 19. I talked about abstinence being the best method of prevention, and I will continue to emphasize that important fact.

All information will be medically and factually accurate according to Missouri State Statute 170.015.1.

Parkway School District Board Policy invites parents to pull out their son or daughter if they choose an abstinence-only curriculum. This will not have a negative impact on the student's grade.

Therefore, if you would like for your son or daughter to **NOT** attend class on May 14–19, please sign below, and I will give him or her an abstinence-only assignment to work on in the counseling loft right outside my room instead of seeing the videos.

Ms. Roper

Do NOT return this form if you DO want your son or daughter to have the Parkway lessons on Disease Prevention and Healthful Relationships.

- -

Sign here if (and only if) you want me to give your son or daughter an alternative assignment to the Parkway School District lessons.

Student name _____

Block _____

Parent name _____

Talking with Your Student's Teachers about Sexuality

There is more talk about sexual issues in school than what occurs in sex education classes. Teachers and kids alike commonly discuss what happens every day in hallways and classrooms. In fact, we hope that teachers will take teachable moments, teach the kids a fact, reinforce a value, or practice a communication skill, and then explain specifically why the current situation requires a classroom chat.

While we hope that our teachers are addressing sexuality education as a normal part of the school experience, you might wonder when you should call the teacher about a sexual issue. If you think the teacher would like to know what your child said about the classroom conversation, by all means, call. It can be very helpful to teachers to get immediate feedback, especially when a sexual subject is the topic. You might be concerned for any number of reasons about what your child reported. Maybe it sounds as though a "dirty" joke was told by a student or even the teacher. Perhaps the teacher explained something in a way your child didn't understand.

If you decide to talk with the teacher, here are a few pointers on how to make sure it goes smoothly:

- **Call at the end of the school day.**
- **If you call and get a voice mailbox, just ask that the teacher call you.** Leave a couple of telephone numbers, such as your cell and home number.
- **When you do have the conversation, make sure your child is not listening.**
- **Report to the teacher what your child told you, and tell her why you are calling.** For example: "Hi, this is Alex's mom/dad. Do you have a minute to chat? I'd like to tell you something that Alex told me yesterday. I thought I would call you and let you tell me about it."
- **Listen to the teacher. Take notes.**
- **If you are pleased with what the teacher says, then you can thank her for creating an askable classroom and affirm that you support her in making sexuality a natural part of students' learning.** You may want to call the principal and compliment the teacher.
- **If you are not pleased with what you hear, then tell her that you are concerned and why.** Be calm and specific.
- **Be clear about what you want the teacher to do.** For example, "In the future, I'd like for you to come down harder on those students who are asking personal questions." Or, if it is his or her opinion you disagreed with, "In the future, would you please be more clear that what you are going to say is your personal opinion and that other reasonable people have opposing views?"
- **At some point in the conversation, say that you will think about what she has said and call back next week if you are still concerned.** Then follow through with another chat with the teacher before you call the principal.
- **Think carefully about what you want from the situation.** Maybe the phone call alone can make things better. Maybe you want the future program for other people's kids to be changed. This will help you focus your comments. If you want your child to be pulled out of the current program, then ask that the teacher be sensitive to his feelings by not making a big deal out of your child's disappearance during the lessons.

This handout may be reproduced for educational, noncommercial uses only (with this copyright line). From *Healthy Teen Relationships: Using Values and Choices to Teach Sex Education* by Martha R. Roper. Copyright © 2011 by Search Institute®, Minneapolis, Minnesota, 877-240-7251 ext. 1, www.search-institute.org. All rights reserved.

Endnotes

1. U.S. Department of Health and Human Services, Administration for Children and Families, Administration on Children, Youth and Families, Children's Bureau, *Child Maltreatment 2008,* available from www.acf.hhs.gov/programs/cb/stats_research/index.htm#can, 2010.

2. Kirby, Douglas, *Emerging Answers 2007: Research Findings on Programs to Reduce Teen Pregnancy and Sexually Transmitted Diseases,* Washington, DC: National Campaign to Prevent Teen and Unplanned Pregnancy, 2007.

3. Ibid.

4. Ibid.

5. Haffner, Debra, Ed., *Guidelines for Comprehensive Sexuality Education, Kindergarten–12th grade.* New York: Sex Information and Education Council of the United States, 1991.

6. The Joint Committee on National Health Education Standards, *National Health Education Standards: Achieving Excellence* (2nd Edition), Atlanta: American Cancer Society, 2007.

Chapter 2

Planning for Sexuality Education

While there is ongoing debate about the best style of lesson planning, there is no debate that there must be a plan for parents and administrators to see and approve. All curricula require that teachers write out what they intend to teach, from the big vision all the way down to what they want students to know and be able to do and how they plan to teach it. In sex education, we want students' values to improve as well. As discussed before, the research of Douglas Kirby shows that there are several characteristics of effective sex education. It is proven that curricula that faithfully follow the characteristics of effective sex education can change not only knowledge, but also values and behavior.

When it comes to planning or teaching the lessons yourself, you need to check to see that you have covered the general lesson plan outline that professionals use. If you are teaching for a school district, you will write plans that follow their plan. If you are teaching for a community group or agency, follow the plan they provide.

REAL THOUGHTS FROM TEENS

"People in school always stop and make out in hallways, and it can get really dirty. Should I say something or just walk on by? Right now I'm just embarrassed."

I wonder sometimes if we who teach sex education have to plan more carefully because people worry that we have a political agenda. It's important for us to examine our personal motives for wanting to teach in this battleground of the American culture wars. Our agendas will become crystal clear to adults and some young people who observe us, so we need to have a commitment to our organizational mission to proceed into this murky swamp. No one will offer us a hand if we step out on the end of a plank by ourselves. Support for our programs requires strong lesson plans.

Setting Up the Room

Sometimes teachers are given lovely rooms that have windows with landscaped views and all the amenities of the Club Level of a five-star hotel. Most of us, however, are given a space with chairs. It is up to us to transform it into a safe and comfortable place to learn.

If you are assigned a room other than your classroom at school, I suggest familiarizing yourself with the room ahead of time. Here is a list of arrangements you may want to discuss with your contact person:

- enough chairs and a table or cart
- access to the Internet
- a projector that can connect to your laptop, set up and ready to go
- the location of restrooms
- basic room supplies such as pencils and paper
- a nametag for yourself
- markers for students to write on blank paper during group work
- healthy snacks, or just bottled water if no healthy snacks are available; if you are teaching in a school, get permission to let students bring bottled water to class
- an attendance list/sign-up sheet in the front of the room
- a seating assignment if you're in a school and you have to take roll
- your framed diploma(s) that shows you are qualified to teach this class
- a personal item such as a family photo or a photo of you accepting an award for a personal or professional accomplishment to show the class during your brief introduction (this could lead to an icebreaker where each person gets out one item from their book bag or wallet and tells why this item is important); if a person does not have a physical item to share, that person may pass or share a favorite TV show, song, movie, or food
- a kitchen timer
- easel and paper (you can bring your own easel with the session agenda already written on it)
- any designated peer leaders and/or co-teachers

Setting up the room means paying attention to how you look and what your first impression will be. Just as we don't want to use shocking words, we also don't want to attract unnecessary attention because of how we look. Each of us is allowed to be who we are and to be proud of that, but think about the first thing the student will say when asked later: What is your teacher like? You do *not* want to be remembered for what you wore to teach a sex education class. So avoid wearing items with logos on them, and be aware that parents might be concerned if you have visible tattoos or if you have any body piercings besides your ears. I would go for the best professional impression possible, because we don't get a second chance to make a first impression.

Group Facilitation Skills

New teachers are concerned about knowing sexuality education content well enough to teach it, but there's another, hidden curriculum: the effective

> A parent called my evaluator and asked why I had told the class that I wear red the morning after my husband and I have sex. She was sure it was true because her son heard this in the lunchroom from his friends at his table. Many hours of embarrassing conversation later, my principal convinced the mom that this was not true. However, the rumor lives on. I no longer wear red to school at all, even though our school colors are red, white, and blue.

management of group dynamics. Styles vary when the class takes place in a school day as opposed to a community or religious setting where students are there by choice. Teachers may vary their styles even within one class period. It depends on the situation, and it's important to talk about that with the class on the first day.

"How do we do things in this sex ed class?" I ask aloud. And I answer my own question with: "We will run this class pretty much like your other classes in school, except that the subject matter is sexuality." I like to establish procedures early in the class so there will be no surprises. Students don't like to be embarrassed, so, as in all classrooms, many housekeeping details are posted and/or mentioned at the beginning. I find that students don't listen well on the first day of class. Adolescents are usually so aware of the other students that they really can't hear you at first. Briefly mentioning the procedures is good enough, and then posting them and walking the students through the system the first few times makes everyone feel more relaxed. Do not be surprised or upset if you find that kids are not listening to you or others. Our minds wander as we connect what we hear to what we think we already know.

REAL THOUGHTS FROM TEENS
"Where is the G-spot?"

Here is a list of what students want to know and what I want them to know. Your own approach may be different.

1. *Where do I sit?* Alphabetically at first. I have a seating chart laid out the first day of class and observe as they help each other find their seats. Late arrivals on the first day are directed by classmates as to where to sit.

2. *What happens when I need to use the restroom? Where is the nearest restroom?* In our school we have a sign-out sheet, and students need to carry a pass. I explain that it's for their safety to leave a paper trail wherever they go.

3. *Where will we go during an emergency?* Your answer will depend on your school's procedures and layout.

4. *Are there items such as tissues, lotion, and hand sanitizer in the room for us to use?* Yes. Show them where they are.

5. *What will we do today?* Have the day's agenda on easel paper where everyone can see it at the beginning of class.

6. *May we speak out without raising our hands?* "Yes, if you are not stepping on someone else's sentence or speaking out too much. Generally, if you are talking more than others, you should hold back. If you don't talk much, you should speak up and share your ideas." Encourage group discussion, and discourage the same person from speaking most of the time.

7. *May we choose our own groups?* "Sometimes. I want you to get to know more people in the class."

8. *May we ask any question whenever we want?* "Yes and no. We have a question box for off-topic questions, and if the question concerns what we are talking about right now, go ahead and ask it. If it turns out to be a complicated answer that we will want to take more time with, then we will write it down on our

list to come back to. We don't want to get too far off track, and I will tell you when I think that is happening." Ask: "Will anyone volunteer to watch the clock and courteously point to it when we are all getting off track?" I find this works well since I sometimes answer an ounce question with a pound answer. Remember to honor the Question Box portion of the class at the end of each session.

9. *Will we ever get to take breaks?* I use "breaks" strategically to transition from one activity to the next. At school we don't take breaks outside the classroom, but out of school it can be a great way to let go of a subject and reassemble for the next topic. At school, I say: "Take a minute to sit quietly or socialize with someone you're sitting next to while I get set up for the next activity."

10. *How will we be graded?* In groups outside of school, there will be no tests and no grades. I am not including a grading system here because the teachers among us know how their own school wants assessments to work. We all know that as soon as we get really good and comfortable with one system, it is changed by the latest educational reform movement, so we stay loose and focused on how our evaluators want to see our results *this* year.

If you find you are losing control, get their attention, smile, and say: "I think I'm losing control!" You can also say: "Wave if you can see me." Then wave and smile. Soon everyone will be waving. Say: "This is how I will get your attention when we need to move on."

If you realize you don't know the answer to a question, just say so and that you will get back to the students about it next time. There is no shame in not knowing an answer to a question.

And don't be afraid to mix things up and change lessons around to keep them fresh. We have many tools in our box of teaching strategies. The following table provides a list to refer to when you're out of ideas or need a new perspective.

> Once I was asked by a fifth grader in an assembly about whether gay men had the same level of testosterone and sperm count as straight men. Out of the corner of my eye, I saw the principal waving his hands above his head trying to tell me not to answer the question. I said I was not sure and that since I was a guest speaker, he would need to ask another adult.

Be careful about your language as well as the students' language. There is a fine line to walk in sexuality education, because the words the students may use to communicate are different from what we think are appropriate for educational settings. When a word is used that I am concerned about, I ask that the students use another word for classroom conversation. Sometimes a word is used that I don't know. I ask for someone to whisper in my ear what it means. I say: "If you don't tell me, I won't know." There is another choice now: when a word is used, I can get out my smartphone and look it up

Teaching Styles: What's in Your Toolbox?

Icebreakers and warm-ups

Lectures

Lecturettes

Interactive lectures

Large-group discussions

Small-group discussions and reports to class

Role modeling skills

Vocabulary skills

Posters and models

Brainstorming

High tech, low tech, and no tech

Role playing

Case studies

Peer-reviewed studies

Outside speakers and guest panels

Peer teaching

Sharing

Interviews

Games

Skill practices

News

Forced choice exercises ("You must choose A or B.")

Continuum exercises ("On a scale of 1 to 10 . . .")

Values voting

Group service projects

Reading aloud

Silent reading

Online videos

Videos

PowerPoint presentations

Music

Journaling

Surveys

Individual student presentations

Group presentations

Group skits

Teacher demonstrations

Student-generated public service announcements (PSAs)

Giving awards and hearing acceptance speeches

Free discussion

Reviewing and summarizing

Pair and share

on the spot. The students and I usually laugh, and the lesson continues as I rephrase or substitute the word in question.

Humor is tricky in class. We want to have a sense of humor about ourselves, but we never want to laugh at others or tell a joke that could be considered "dirty." We can talk about humor and discuss how it can be a wonderful part of life, but that if it's used to hurt others, then it's a bad thing.

> **Humor can be used to teach or to make a point. The story about the 6-year-old whose friend said he found a condom on the veranda and the child asked: "What's a veranda?" is not a dirty joke. It is a commentary on how much children know about sexuality and how much they don't know yet in general.**

When there is a person in the class who wants people to laugh at her comments, it makes it hard to continue with the activity we have planned. Sometimes student comments can provide comic relief, and I can laugh and enjoy having that student speak out. However, if the blurting out does not provide a useful function to the group, then I can ask the person to please wait and be called on to talk. If the remark is inappropriate, I can send an "I" message: "When _____, I feel _____ because I think _____. I would like _____."

When I handle conflict in the group using "I" messages, I provide the students with a good role

When _____
(some specific event occurs)

I feel _____
(some variation of happy, sad, mad, scared)

because I think _____
(a thought or opinion)

I would like _____
(or "I was wondering if . . ." or
"In the future could you . . .?")

model. I do this so consistently that even the students begin to refer to the posted "I" message and fill in the blanks. This provides a good laugh for all as well as the message that the student is trying to get across.

Kids who talk too much to others during class distract from the group experience. I am delighted that students have so much energy and interest in sex education and that they want to pair up and share what they are thinking. However, even in sex education class (and perhaps even more because it's sex education), we cannot have chaos. We want to make sure that our students are learning what we want them to learn.

There are many ways to get private conversations to stop, and the first one is to stop talking while that person is talking. Look at the person. Ask if he wants to share with the class. If not, send an "I" message: "When there is talking while another student is talking, I feel concerned, because I think that others might think their opinion is not valued. I'd like for you to wait to share your thought with everyone." If this doesn't work, then you can stop each time, say the person's name, and wait. I do that several times until I ask the person to wait after class to see if there is something else going on. In school I move the person to a different seat. If lots of side conversations about the topic are starting at once, it means that the kids are all interested in discussing it, so I just say: "This generated lots of energy. Turn to the person next to you and talk about it for a minute or two."

When it appears that a group of students is forming an exclusive club or alliance within the class, it is probably time to move the students around the room for a different project or perhaps talk with that group after class. Sticking with the "I" message format will help model for those students how to communicate their concerns to others.

For example: "When I hear you talk among yourselves, I feel concerned because I think others may think you don't value their opinions. I would like for you to reach out to everyone in the group." I have done this in front of the class when the group cohesion is threatened, and it worked to get the class back on track. It doesn't always work that way.

When there is a person in the group who blurts out with anger or contempt toward another person, I call a time-out for the class to write in their journal, and I ask the offending student to talk privately with me just outside my door. I ask what happened and try to listen without judgment. I also state why the remark was inappropriate and see how that person responds. In school, I might send the person to the

REAL THOUGHTS FROM TEENS

"Is masturbating for half a year [bad] for your health and is it possible for you to have a kid by doing that?"

principal for a conference until the student is ready to apologize to me or the offended student. In a community group, there may be an understanding with the agency or religious group that sponsors the class about what to do if there is a problem. Verbal abuse, bullying, and teasing should be considered a serious threat, and there must be immediate consequences. Make sure you have a plan for that unfortunate situation.

Fostering Caring Relationships

In order to foster caring relationships, there needs to be something special about attending your class. Students need to feel valued and important, and small things such as remembering birthdays, acknowledging accomplishments, and keeping track of milestones can mean a lot.

For example, if you're a health teacher like me, you may want to bring healthy food from time to time. Food is an icebreaker, can sometimes be a good reward, and can sometimes provide a teachable moment about eating. Young people are exposed to non-nutritious food, soda, and candy everywhere they look. The message here is that fueling our bodies with healthy food is as important as fueling our minds with healthy thoughts, and the message the students receive is "I care about you and your health!"

The following are some of the things I do for my homeroom class of 20 students. Depending on how many students you teach, some of these ideas may not be practical, but they may inspire you to find something you *can* do.

- I organize my classes so that relationship building is part of my opening ritual for the day. I like to read inspirational quotes, but you can also just have a casual chat. The main point is for students to recognize that you care about them as people.
- I make a calendar and ask my students to mark their birthdays with their name or initials. I also ask them to bring a sweet snack to share with the class on a student's birthday. I bring a salty snack (usually chips) and an inexpensive birthday card. Then I have the honored student stand up and say how old he is and what that means to him. I usually add the significance that his age has: for example, 16 means a driver's license, 17 means the end of the juvenile legal system, 18 means voting.
- I keep an old-fashioned list of students in a gradebook chart, and write First Call, Second Call, GPA, Birthday, Reading Ability, Summer Postcard, Class Role (e.g., gets attendance ready), Parent Conference, Discipline Issues and Contacts, Other Caring Adults in the Building, and Other Notes. The idea is to see at a glance how well I'm keeping up with my homeroom students, and who can help me.
- I take photos of each student. I get students' approval before I print and post the photos on the wall next to my desk. When all students are present on the same day, I arrange a group photo and send it to their parents and our administrators as a seasonal greeting.

- I hand out index cards to the students and ask them which traditions they want to hold on to, which they would like to let go of, and which they would like to add to our homeroom. I read them out loud and we discuss them.
- I make several sheets of name and address labels of my homeroom kids and mail them postcards, photos, and a separate party invitation for the first day of school.

Handling Awkward Moments

Let's say a student asks you a question like: "How many calories does 'cum' have?" You may think this won't happen, but it did to me on the first day of class one semester. All the other students stared at the student with stunned silence. Then they looked at me.

I said: "Before I answer your question, I think it's a good idea to talk about how to ask questions that might make some people uncomfortable—like this one. It's not a bad question, and some people want to know the answer, but first we will look at the question itself. Frankly, I worry that the students in the class will only remember that you asked this question. Picture this: Your family is at the dinner table tonight, and Dad says: 'So, what did you learn on the first day of school?' If you say that a girl asked the teacher how many calories are in 'cum,' wouldn't that be embarrassing for everybody?"

The students laughed. "Therefore, I have a request. Would you be willing to write that question down on an index card, put it in the Question Box, and wait until we get to that lesson?" She said she would. I added: "If you're asking for a friend who is on a diet or for a friend who's an athlete, then stop by after class and I'll say more. I hesitate to tell you to Google it, because I have Googled that question and I went through ten incorrect answers and silly comments before I began to get to good sources. In this class, we will talk about what good sources are when the topic is sexuality. For today, I will give you www.medlineplus.gov." I went on to introduce the class and begin Lesson 1.

On her way out the door, I said to the curious student, "I worry that people will remember you for the question you asked," and then paused. She said she was not trying to be funny—that she just wanted to know. I said I was concerned that people would think certain things about her and tell others, and then rumors would start and people she didn't even know, the "mean girls" and the bullies, could give her a hard time. "So," I said, "I ask that in the future, please write down questions like that for the Question Box. And if you want to know today, the answer is around 5 to 10 calories."

It is important to answer questions in a way that respects all students present that day. As the semester unfolded, I realized that the girl who asked the question in the first five minutes of class loved to bring attention of this sexual nature to herself. I sent her to her counselor several times to talk about the concerns I had. Although she was able to pull back somewhat, she still needed monitoring and a private conversation after class on many occasions.

REAL THOUGHTS FROM TEENS

"Can you use your cell phone as a vibrator? I heard there are apps for that."

Warm-up Activities

When students walk into the room and sit down, it helps to have a short activity—not related to sex ed—that brings the focus to each other rather than what just happened on the way to class. You want the students to feel comfortable about being in this room, and give them some other things to think about rather than the personal problems they walked in with. Here are a few quick ones:

- Ask students to turn to the person next to them and figure out one thing they have in common. When everyone is done, have that dyad turn to another dyad and figure out what they all have in common. Keep adding another group until pairs become one big group searching for one thing everyone has in common.
- Let each person say one thing she would want to have with her if she were marooned on a deserted island.
- Let each person say what he would do if it were possible to be a benevolent dictator and wave a magic wand to help the world be a better place.
- Make a short list of experiences, places, or birthdays and have students walk around to find someone who has done those things, has gone to those places, or has that birthday. Usually these games are created on a bingo-like paper.
- Have each student find another student in the room who values something that she also admires (for example, courage, friendship, wisdom, justice, honesty, caring, forgiveness). When that person finds someone who agrees, they can try together to convince someone else to join them.
- Have students teach each other one movement—a dance move, a stretch, or a shadow puppet.
- Tell a clean joke.
- Ask students: "What is your favorite comfort food? Where do you want to travel in the world? Where do you *not* want to travel in the world? What song do you like that no one would ever guess about you? What's your favorite TV show or movie? What makes you laugh? Which do you like better: peanut butter or jelly? What's something good about yourself?"
- Ask someone to name everyone in the room.
- Line everyone up by birthday.
- Have students introduce themselves with their names and an adjective that starts with the same letter: David—Dancing David.

Assessment Ideas

Some of you need to give grades, and some may simply want to find out whether what you are teaching is what your students are learning. I have listed some ideas I have found to be successful. You could have students:

- Keep notes/journal with reflections.
- Take true/false pre- and post-tests.

- Write a paragraph summary about what you just said to the class.
- Report to the class about the chapter or paragraph of an article the class read.
- Interview parents as part of a homework assignment and write up the interview.
- Make a poster to preach or teach ("Don't TEXT and Drive!").
- Work on a group report.
- Show use of skills through role play.
- Develop news reports from two articles, giving clear citations from two good sources.
- Participate in a group project to make a news report about a topic.
- Participate in a group project to make up a role play about a topic showing two ways to solve a dilemma.
- Make and present a PowerPoint.
- Have each student sign up on a self-help website that tracks specific behaviors students want to add or modify. Lance Armstrong's website, www.livestrong.com, allows students to take a dare to improve their relationship skills. It is an assignment that one student can demonstrate in front of the class by signing up, finding the relationship dares, and then beginning the charting process for the class to see and discuss. Students can then intentionally add a simple health skill into their day, chart it, and print it to turn in for points or a group discussion.
- Go to www.rubistar4teachers.org for a free source of assessment ideas.
- Go to puzzle.com for puzzles that can be used for warm-up activities.
- Take traditional tests. If you are teaching for a school that has to have a certain percentage of the test questions the same, then make sure you tell the students clearly what you are testing them on and then do that.
- Make public service announcements with a video camera.

What to Do Each Session

The following is a checklist for each classroom session:

___Smiles and Greetings by Name

___Quick Warm-up Activity

___Sexuality News of the Day

___Introduction of the Lesson

___The Lesson

___Group Activity

___Group Work

___Reports to Large Group and Class Discussion

___Question Box

___Summary by Teacher and Students

___Reflections in Journal

Characteristics of Effective Sex Education Checklist

Douglas Kirby created a list of effective characteristics of sex education that I have turned into the following checklist. You can review this checklist regularly to make sure your emphasis stays on what works in sex education.

___I am trained and ready to teach this lesson.

___I have the support I need in teaching this lesson.

___This lesson is age appropriate.

___This lesson is culturally appropriate.

___The participants feel socially safe to participate.

___The parents and community feel comfortable with the lesson.

___The emphasis is on values (and good choices.)

___I am developing students' communication skills.

___I am developing students' refusal skills.

___I am developing students' negotiation skills.

___I am providing medically accurate information about abstinence.

___I am providing medically accurate information about contraception, condoms, and Plan B.

___I state clear goals for preventing HIV, other STIs, and/or teen pregnancy.

___I focus on specific health behaviors related to these goals, with clear messages about these behaviors using role play for practice.

___I address psychosocial risk and protective factors (assets) with activities to change each targeted risk and to promote each protective factor.

___I respect the state law, the community values, and the community needs.

___I rely on participatory teaching methods.[1]

Endnote

1. Kirby, Douglas, *Emerging Answers 2007: Research Findings on Programs to Reduce Teen Pregnancy and Sexually Transmitted Diseases*, Washington, DC: National Campaign to Prevent Teen and Unplanned Pregnancy, 2007.

Chapter 3

Questions, Answers, and Opinions

The following activities can be used as part of your class routine or as fillers when there is extra time. I like to start each day with quiet reflective time that a reading provides, followed by the **Question Box** activity. A review of the last class and a quick overview of what you'll cover that day helps orient the students to the next lesson.

It's also a good idea to set up ground rules and decide on conflict management strategies right from the start, and the **Ground Rules** and **Ouch/Oops** and **Meaning of Sex** activities in this chapter are designed to help each class set boundaries and expectations, so that everyone is aware of the kinds of behavior and speech that are welcomed or discouraged. Finally, the **Asset Building with Values & Choices** activity gives students space to explore how they feel about sex and express themselves in a safe space.

If you would like to connect your curriculum more directly to Search Institute's Developmental Assets, the Asset Building with Values & Choices activity gives you the opportunity to discuss the Developmental Assets in terms of how they apply to healthy relationships and sexual decisions. This activity lays the groundwork for exploring the assets throughout the rest of the class sessions.

> **REAL THOUGHTS FROM TEENS**
>
> "How can you tell the difference between someone who really likes you versus just sexually?"

The Question Box

Question

What do kids really want to know when they take a sex education class?

General Objective

Students can ask a question by writing it down anonymously and putting it in the Question Box.

Measurable Objective

Students will ask a question by writing it down anonymously and putting it in the Question Box.

Time and Materials

- 15 to 30 minutes
- A box with a hole cut in the top, a hat or basket, or other receptacle
- Two packs of 3" x 5" index cards

Instructions

Tell students you understand that they may have questions that don't come up in the lessons we have planned for them. Therefore, you have created a Question Box. Leave a whole package of blank index cards in the box, and give each student three cards to keep in their notebooks so they can write down their questions as they occur to them. Remind them to write with black or blue pen and to change their writing style so no one will recognize their handwriting. Ask them to be courteous in posing their questions, and assure them that you will do your best to protect everyone from embarrassment.

Invite students to write one question right away to demonstrate how the questions will be handled throughout the class.

Have students write one or more questions on a card. Look the other way while they are writing, and as you collect the cards, stand an arm's length away from students as they put their questions in the box. Suggest to them that they not fold them so everyone's question cards will look the same on the outside. Mix the cards or shake the box as you walk around the room to assure students that you do not want to know whose card belongs to whom. Suggest to students who say they don't have a question that they turn in a blank card this one time so others won't feel silly for having questions.

After all have turned in one card, pick the cards up and start going through them to see what kinds of questions this group has. When I have several classes, I use a specific color of card for each class so the same students who wrote the question will hear the answer.

Read a question and answer it briefly. If students seem really interested in the question and answer, try to provide as much information as you can. Confirm that you have answered the question by asking for follow-up questions.

Remind students of the process of being able to ask questions anonymously and tell them that you will start each class with the routine of answering a few questions, keeping the lesson starting and ending time in mind.

Notes

If a question seems as if it could be a cry for help (such as, "What do you do if you think you have an STI?"), pause before your answer and emphasize to the class how important it is to have adult help in such situations. Tell them to talk to one adult after another until they find someone who will help them. Assure the class that you are a good person to start with, and you are always available to talk privately.

I leave last year's questions in the box and read them as examples so students will know what other kids asked. That generates lots of questions, and it reassures students that I am an "askable" teacher who does not judge the person by the question. If you do not have questions from previous years, you can make up some of your own.

I usually pick one polite question to answer, and one rude question. The polite question is generally easy to answer. For example, it might read: "Can a girl get pregnant the first time she has sex?" (Yes, even before menarche, or first menstruation.) A rude question is more difficult, because you do not want to discourage questions, but you want to let the students know that you will rephrase questions that you know from experience will embarrass some people. A question that seems intended to get a laugh can be rephrased to bore even the most interested student.

With questions like "How do you give a good blowjob?" or "Should girls peel and eat bananas in the school cafeteria?" you can assume that the questioner is having fun without concern for others' feelings. They may be unaware that they are creating an uncomfortable situation that can embarrass people to the point of not wanting to participate in the class anymore. It's not bad to have these questions, but asking them in public—even on an anonymous card in a sex ed class—may cause others to rethink taking the class depending on how the teacher answers the questions.

When you run into such questions, I suggest telling the class what I explained before about making the class uncomfortable, and that those kinds of questions are more like "questments": statements that are posed as a question, but are really intended to make a statement. Sexual techniques and sexual jokes are not a part of the curriculum. However, if a student really wants to know the answer to a serious question, that individual should arrange a time after class to talk about it. If the issues brought up require a referral, then you can write a hall pass or walk the student to a counselor or principal right at that moment.

If the questions embarrass you, the teacher, then look online for more information. And if you are still not sure what to do about the answer, ask your mentors and your evaluator for advice.

Students who ask questions like these in class may also add to the story at their lunch table, and then a rumor is born about you, the teacher, that might get woven into the class lore for generations. You do not want this to happen—it's not good public relations for the human sexuality class you are trying so hard to make a part of your larger curriculum—but you can't always prevent it. There is really no way to avoid rumors and stories about you when you teach anything with the word "sex" in it. Supportive people have always told me that if people are talking about the class, I must be doing something right.

> **REAL THOUGHTS FROM TEENS**
> "Is masturbation considered healthy at any age? Even older adults?"

Ground Rules and "Ouch/Oops"

Question

How will we talk with each other? How will we treat each other in this course as we talk about sexuality?

General Objective

This lesson provides the opportunity to set a comfortable tone and establish an atmosphere of respect and openness. It teaches students how to manage conflict around sexual issues.

Measurable Objective

Students will be able to demonstrate an example of an "Ouch" and an "Oops" and explain the process of sensitive communication.

Time and Materials

- 30 minutes
- A 3" x 5" index card for each student
- Easel paper, markers, and tape to post the class guidelines

Instructions

There are two parts to this lesson:

1. Setting ground rules
2. Agreeing on how to solve group conflict quickly with the "Ouch/Oops" method.

Part 1. Start by giving a short talk about the sex education class that the students are going to take. It may sound something like this:

"We are going to be talking about human sexuality. Your parents want you to have information about this important area of your life to help you become more comfortable with this sensitive topic. You've been given so many conflicting messages about sex that it's a good idea to sit together for a few sessions and go over what is being said, what we know to be true, what we believe about sexuality, and how we should make decisions. It all boils down to our values and our choices, which is the name of this course.

"The first thing we will need to do as a group is to decide together how we will talk and act in this room. You are used to having group guidelines in school classes, so this will not be hard to do. However, the subject of sexuality can make people feel uncomfortable, so we will want to think about our rules of communication very carefully. We want to build empathy and to be sensitive to each other. We will continue to come back to the importance of respecting each other and managing our conflicts because it's normal to disagree with each other. We have a right to our own opinions, but we don't have a right to show disrespect to each other. Let's get started on our list of group norms."

Then invite your students to generate a list of dos and don'ts for the group in order for everyone to feel safe. Feeling safe helps build empathy and sensitivity—values that promote good habits in all relationships.

Students might suggest things like this:

Turn off cell phones and other electronic devices.

Be a good listener.

People have the right to their own opinions.

No put-downs.

It's okay to laugh with people, but not at them.

Respect each other's privacy (don't ask personal questions and don't tell your sexual secrets).

No one has to share personal opinions.

Maintain confidentiality in the group.

Speak from your own experience.

Accept each other.

Listen with curiosity to learn.

Remain on task.

Start and end on time.

Write all the suggestions on easel paper so you can post them on the wall for the duration of the course.

Part 2. Write on easel paper a list of topics that people need to be aware of in getting along with others successfully. For example: age; sex, gender, sexual identity, and sexual orientation; race; religion; ethnic and national origin; family income; family education; physical appearance; physical ability and/or disability; mental ability and/or disability; invisible differences.

Explain why it's important to be respectful of each of the things on this list. Then you may want to say something like this:

"The second way we will build empathy and sensitivity in this group is to agree to a process we call 'Ouch and Oops.' The idea is that often people offend each other without meaning to. We are a diverse group, and we don't have to agree with each other. However, we do need to stop saying things that are offensive to others and keep participants from feeling safe. So if someone makes a comment that another person finds hurtful or offensive, that person can say 'Ouch' and explain why he found that comment hurtful. For instance, if someone says 'That's so gay,' then someone else could say 'Ouch.' The conversation would stop and the person who said it would say, 'Why is that an ouch for you?' The other person would let the group know what was offensive about what was said. After the explanation or further discussion, the person who said 'That's so gay,' would say 'Oops.' Everyone can take a deep breath and move on with the lesson."

Ask students to role play how to use the Ouch/Oops method to avoid stepping on someone's toes. Give students index cards and ask them to write a list of common put-downs that are heard at school, around friends, and online. Pull out the ones that are inappropriate for this lesson. Then divide students into groups to create role plays. Give them five minutes. Walk around to see that they are on track with showing each other how to say "Ouch" and "Oops."

Finally, lead a discussion to summarize and to get closure on the topic of building empathy and sensitivity while discussing sexual issues. Keep the conversation light and encouraging as though you have confidence that they all want to get along, but that sometimes we all make mistakes in how our words come out. Assure them that trust will develop as we practice the "Ouch/Oops" method to develop cultural competence.

Notes

You may also want to suggest that the objecting student use an "I" message (discussed in chapter 2): When _____, I feel _____ because I think _____. I would like_____.

So the "I" message would go something like this: "When you say 'That's so gay,' I feel offended because I think that is a put-down on all gay people. I would like for us not to use put-downs so everyone feels safe to be who they are in this class."

If the original speaker does not accept the "I" message, then more discussion needs to take place, perhaps after the class. However, when students see the method used and see that it works, people are less likely to get defensive when someone says "Ouch."

The Meaning of Sex

Question
What does the word "sex" mean?

General Objective
The word "sex" is hard to define, and this activity helps expand everyone's vocabulary and understanding of sexuality to try to communicate more clearly, maturely, and politely about this complicated topic.

Measurable Objective
Students will be able to draw the Circles of Sexuality and fill in at least three appropriate words within each circle.

Time and Materials
- 45 minutes
- Easel pad, markers, and tape
- Circles of Sexuality handout
- 3" x 5" index cards with sexual words, phrases, and behaviors on them

Instructions
Explain that most of us are pretty familiar with the word "sex," and that we have a pretty good idea about what it means. There are many languages of sexuality: there is street language, language we use at home, language we use with friends, and the educational language of sexuality, which is what we will use in this class. If students don't know the proper medical term or accepted word, they may say their own version in order to learn what to replace it with.

Tell the class that so many people define the word "sex" differently that it has become important to use clear words to describe behavior, intimacy, sexual identity, sexual health, reproduction, sexualization, or sensuality. Invite the class to look at a diagram that helps divide the components of sexuality into several areas, so that they can make sure they talk in ways everyone understands.

> **REAL THOUGHTS FROM TEENS**
>
> **"Is homosexuality a choice?"**

Lead students through a short tour of the Circles of Sexuality. Draw the circles with their headings on easel paper, and begin to describe a category, such as Intimacy. Fill in some of the words you discuss, such as *caring* and *sharing*. Invite the students to join in. Pass out the index cards with words and phrases written on them, and then have students hold them up and guess which circle(s) they belong in.

The Circles of Sexuality

Sexuality encompasses nearly every aspect of our being, from attitudes and values to feelings and experiences. It is influenced by the individual, family, culture, religion/spirituality, laws, professions, institutions, science, and politics.

Sensuality
Skin hunger
Aural/visual stimuli
Sexual response cycle
Body image
Fantasy

Sexualization
Flirting
Media messages/images
Seduction
Withholding sex
Sexual harassment
Incest
Rape

Intimacy
Caring
Sharing
Loving/liking
Risk taking
Vulnerability
Self-disclosure
Trust

VALUES

Sexual Health and Reproduction
Sexual behavior
Anatomy and physiology
Sexual/reproductive systems
Contraception/abortion
Sexually transmitted infections

Sexual Identity
Biological gender
Gender identity
Gender role
Sexual orientation

Sexualization involves how we use our sexuality and may include manipulating or controlling others. Its components are media images/messages, flirting, seduction, withholding sex, sexual harassment, incest, and rape.

Sexual health and reproduction relates to attitudes and behaviors toward our health and the consequences of sexual activity. Its components are behavior, anatomy and physiology, sexually transmitted infection, contraception, and abortion (spontaneous or induced).

Sensuality involves our level of awareness, acceptance, and enjoyment of our own or others' bodies.

Sexual identity is how we perceive ourselves as sexual beings. Its components are biological gender, gender identity, gender role, and sexual orientation.

Intimacy is the degree to which we express and have a need for closeness with another person. Its components are caring, sharing, liking/loving, trust, vulnerability, self-disclosure, and emotional risk taking.

This handout may be reproduced for educational, noncommercial uses only (with this copyright line). From *Healthy Teen Relationships: Using Values and Choices to Teach Sex Education* by Martha R. Roper. Copyright © 2011 by Search Institute®, Minneapolis, Minnesota, 877-240-7251 ext. 1, www.search-institute.org. All rights reserved. Adapted from a model designed by Dennis Dailey, Ph.D. Used with permission.

Be encouraging with all words, but also explain that we are going to talk in the adult language of sexuality, not slang terms, and certainly not derogatory terms. However, if a word comes up that does offend someone, it is a good time to practice the Ouch/Oops method of communication. Misunderstanding and conflict are normal in this sensitive and personal part of our lives.

Give each student a handout with the Circles of Sexuality filled in. They can add new words if they like. Invite the students to turn to each other and explain what the Circles of Sexuality mean. Or, divide students into small groups and have each student in the group be responsible for explaining one circle to the rest of the group.

Conclude by summarizing how complicated sexuality is and invite students to improve their vocabulary when talking about sexuality in this class—and elsewhere.

Notes

Sometimes a student will want to use inappropriate language or ask inappropriate questions just to get attention. You can ask students to put a question in the Question Box, or you can help them rephrase the question to demonstrate the point of the lesson: that they learn to respect others' feelings of safety and comfort in the group. It's important to protect all group members—even the person who is insensitive to others. A quiet, private moment with the student after class will help set the tone for future class discussions.

Asset Building with Values and Choices

Question

What do students need to know about sexual values and choices to be successful in high school and beyond?

General Objective

Students will analyze their own assets and write their personal goals relating to all values and choices, but these will include sexual values and choices. Writing down the goals will improve the likelihood of achieving those goals.

Measurable Objective

Students will fill out the Assets Handout and count up their current Assets. They will use the handout to write three personal goals on the back of the paper.

Time and Materials

- Entire class session
- Asset Framework handout (see introduction)
- Asset Checklist handout
- Paper, writing utensils, colored markers
- 3" x 5" index cards

Instructions

Give students a short introduction to the Developmental Assets and distribute the Asset Framework handout. Remind students that personal goals affect sexual choices. For

An Asset Checklist

Many people find it helpful to use a simple checklist to reflect on the assets young people experience. This checklist simplifies the asset list to help prompt conversation in families, organizations, and communities. NOTE: This checklist is not intended nor appropriate as a scientific or accurate measurement of Developmental Assets.

☐ 1. I receive high levels of love and support from family members.

☐ 2. I can go to my parent(s) or guardian(s) for advice and support and have frequent, in-depth conversations with them.

☐ 3. I know some nonparent adults I can go to for advice and support.

☐ 4. My neighbors encourage and support me.

☐ 5. My school provides a caring, encouraging environment.

☐ 6. My parent(s) or guardian(s) help me succeed in school.

☐ 7. I feel valued by adults in my community.

☐ 8. I am given useful roles in my community.

☐ 9. I serve in the community one hour or more each week.

☐ 10. I feel safe at home, at school, and in the neighborhood.

☐ 11. My family sets standards for appropriate conduct and monitors my whereabouts.

☐ 12. My school has clear rules and consequences for behavior.

☐ 13. Neighbors take responsibility for monitoring my behavior.

☐ 14. Parent(s) and other adults model positive, responsible behavior.

☐ 15. My best friends model responsible behavior.

☐ 16. My parent(s)/guardian(s) and teachers encourage me to do well.

☐ 17. I spend three hours or more each week in lessons or practice in music, theater, or other arts.

☐ 18. I spend three hours or more each week in school or community sports, clubs, or organizations.

☐ 19. I spend one hour or more each week in religious services or participating in spiritual activities.

☐ 20. I go out with friends with nothing special to do two or fewer nights each week.

☐ 21. I want to do well in school.

☐ 22. I am actively engaged in learning.

☐ 23. I do an hour or more of homework each school day.

☐ 24. I care about my school.

☐ 25. I read for pleasure three or more hours each week.

☐ 26. I believe it is really important to help other people.

☐ 27. I want to help promote equality and reduce world poverty and hunger.

☐ 28. I can stand up for what I believe.

☐ 29. I tell the truth even when it's not easy.

☐ 30. I can accept and take personal responsibility.

☐ 31. I believe it is important not to be sexually active or to use alcohol or other drugs.

☐ 32. I am good at planning ahead and making decisions.

☐ 33. I am good at making and keeping friends.

☐ 34. I know and am comfortable with people of different cultural/racial/ethnic backgrounds.

☐ 35. I can resist negative peer pressure and dangerous situations.

☐ 36. I try to resolve conflict nonviolently.

☐ 37. I believe I have control over many things that happen to me.

☐ 38. I feel good about myself.

☐ 39. I believe my life has a purpose.

☐ 40. I am optimistic about my future.

This handout may be reproduced for educational, noncommercial uses only (with this copyright line). From *Healthy Teen Relationships: Using Values and Choices to Teach Sex Education* by Martha R. Roper. Copyright © 2011 by Search Institute®, Minneapolis, Minnesota, 877-240-7251 ext. 1, www.search-institute.org. All rights reserved. This checklist is not intended for use as a survey tool.

example, teens who are parents in high school are not likely to graduate from college. College graduates are healthier, make more money, and live longer.

Read a list of sexual choices that high school students need to make:

- How am I supposed to act?
- How am I supposed to dress?
- How do I treat people who are different from me—gay, straight, trans, other?
- How much information do I put on my Internet sites?
- What age is the right age to have sex?
- What are you supposed to know before you have sex?
- How are kids supposed to know how to be in relationships when all they see looks messed up or perfect from the outside?

Tell students that we will be talking about these questions, but there are no magic bullet answers that fit everyone. Values are internal. You cannot see them, although they drive your choices in decision making every minute of every day.

Now hand out the Asset Checklist and let students mark their own assets. Ask them to not take too long to make their checkmarks, and that if they can't answer a simple yes or no, they should move on to the next statement. Tell them that they don't have to discuss personal issues in the class, but that they can make general comments about how assets can help achieve personal goals like going to college and waiting to make life choices like starting a family.

After the Asset Checklist is complete, ask students to turn to the person next to them and reflect on their results. Ask them to talk with each other about what values and choices they might think would influence their sexual decision making. Then ask them to share with the group. Take their sharing as opportunities to further explain what assets are and how students can nurture them and make them a stronger and more positive influence in their lives. Finally, connect the student comments to choices adolescents need to make regarding their sexual lives.

REAL THOUGHTS FROM TEENS

"I heard masturbation makes your penis bigger—is this true or false?"

Now, go back to the Asset Checklist and ask students to pick an internal asset on which they feel they could draw. The students should write the asset and then create a visual that shows its meaning. Students will post their drawings and explain to the class what the visual demonstrates.

Write "Values" on easel paper that will be posted each session. Ask students to list the positive values that were stressed in this session and write them on the easel paper. Then write "Choices" on another sheet of easel paper. Ask students for good choices that we are reminded of that will bring us healthier sexual relationships, and write those down.

Remind students that our sexual decisions need the same serious and thoughtful attention as our college choices and other important life decisions. We will talk openly about these values and choices in upcoming sessions.

Chapter 4

Sexuality and Reality

The activities in this chapter are about how sexuality operates in the real world, encouraging students to think about sexuality not just as an abstract topic, but as something that affects their daily lives.

REAL THOUGHTS FROM TEENS

"Why would a guy want to become a girl?"

The first activity, "Definitions," explores the meaning behind the words we use to describe sexual orientation. That flows naturally into the next lesson, "Gender, Orientation, and Sexuality," where students will discuss how gender relates to sexual orientation. Then "Dress Codes and Body Art" talks about how we express ourselves sexually through what we wear, while "*A* is for Abstinence" helps students talk about what abstinence really means to them and the ramifications of putting it into practice. Finally, "Exploring the Options" gives students space to think about and discuss what they might do when faced with an unplanned pregnancy.

Definitions

Question

What is the difference between gender, sexual expression, and sexual orientation?

General Objective

Students will learn to define various related vocabulary words, differentiate between gender roles, sexual expression, and sexual orientation, and learn why saying things like "That's so gay" can be rude and hurtful.

Measurable Objective

Students will be able to write the definitions of *gay, lesbian, bisexual, straight,* and *transgender.*

Time and Materials

- 30 minutes
- Large poster paper, tape, and markers
- Small squishy ball for throwing to, not at, other students

Instructions

Have students write down what they think of when they hear the following words: *gay, lesbian, bisexual, straight,* and *transgender.* After the students have written their thoughts, have them turn and share what they've written with the person next to them, and explain how they learned or thought of those words.

Now ask students to share what they've written on their papers. Choose students to write their associations with the words on the large poster paper, a different student for each word.

Ask: "What do you notice about the words? Which are kind? Which are unkind? What do the words make you think of? Which are accurate and which are not? Let's circle the ones that make sense to you."

Then read aloud the correct definitions below. (Note: If your school district, state, or province requires you to use different definitions of these terms, read those instead.)

Gay
A gay person is someone—usually a man, although the term can be applied to women—whose primary interest socially, emotionally, psychologically, and sexually is in another man or men, whether or not it's overtly expressed.

Lesbian
A lesbian is a woman whose primary interest socially, emotionally, psychologically, and sexually is in another woman or women, whether or not it's overtly expressed.

Bisexual
Bisexual people have the capacity to feel attracted to others where sex or gender is not necessarily the defining factor.

Straight
A straight person is a man or woman whose primary interest is in another person or persons of the other gender, whether or not it's overtly expressed.

Trans or Transgender
A transgender person is someone whose gender identity—the inner feeling that we are a man or a woman, masculine or feminine—is different from the way his or her biological body looks and functions.

Now ask students what they notice about these definitions, and pose the following questions for discussion:

- Are these people interested in just sex with another person?
- What does "whether or not they are overtly expressed" mean?
- Why do gay people, lesbians, bisexual people, and trans people get put down?
- What are some ways we put down gay people, lesbians, bisexual people, and trans people?
- Who puts down others? (No names here. Remember, in this class we don't use names or identifiable details.) What are the characteristics of a person who puts others down, bullies, or teases them?
- What makes people put them down?
- What are some examples?

Now take the squishy ball and throw it to someone. Ask him the definition of *lesbian*. Tell him to say as much as he remembers and then toss the ball to someone else to complete it. When that student completes it, she can toss the ball to someone else and ask him to define another word, until the students become more facile with the definitions.

If time allows, you can also add the following:

Exit Slip

In the last few minutes of class, ask the students to fill out an "exit slip" and hand it to you on their way out. You can prepare the slips ahead of time or just read the following questions out loud:

- What was the takeaway from today?
- What do you remember that's most important?
- What do you want to change in your behavior as a result of this lesson?

Short Videos

Show three videos from a current anti-bullying campaign. You may need to show each one twice; the students might miss the message, because in some videos the actors speak quickly and the clips are over so fast.

In small groups, ask the students to write down what these three videos are trying to show and how they are trying to show that message.

- How frequently do you say "That's so gay"?
- How frequently do some of your friends say, "Oh, that's so gay"?
- What could stop your friends or people you know from saying that?
- If you hear others saying, "That's so gay" in the future, what could you say?

Notes

This is a lesson from my colleague Judith Steinhart, a health educator and consultant (judithsteinhart.com and heyjud.com). I have included it here with permission because the subject of bullying is often given to health and sex ed teachers, and because our values and choices are never clearer and more observable than when we stand up for a friend or acquaintance—or especially a stranger.

Gender, Orientation, and Sexuality

Question

How is sexuality related to our gender and orientation?

General Objective

Students will understand how sexuality is related to our gender and orientation.

Measurable Objective

Students will be able to define what it means to be transgender.

REAL THOUGHTS FROM TEENS

"Last year the boys behind me in math always talked about sex and what they had done or planned on doing. What should I have done?"

Time and Materials
- 15 to 30 minutes
- Transgender handout

Instructions

First, start with a quick review of the anatomy and physiology of the male and female sexual systems.

Now say something like: "Most people are born with obviously male or clear female body parts, but sometimes their physical sex isn't clear at birth or a person begins to notice that their body or their feelings about their body is not like most people who identify as a male or female. The term for this is *trans* or *transgender*. This condition can occur due to hormones or genes or an unknown reason. Almost everyone can experience sexual pleasure, and almost everyone wants to share it with a partner at some point in their lives. Some people want to get married and have children. Some do not."

Then pass out the "When a Person Says She or He Is Transgender" handout (page 59). Read the headings out loud. Remind students that this might be a conversation that could make people uncomfortable, but that being uncomfortable is not bad. It may be necessary to feel the feelings in order to understand something different from what you have heard before. It is a good time to talk about the fact that there is no public place where we can be rude and mean to "them" because "they" are part of the public and may be in this very room at this very moment. Everyone deserves to be treated with respect at all times.

Say: "While knowing about sexual anatomy and physiology is important, it is much more important to make good choices in our sexual lives. What are some words and body parts that you might need to say out loud in the future with your partner or your doctor? Since most people want to express their sexual feelings with a partner, it is important to be able to talk about sexual anatomy and physiology, sexual response, and sexual identity."

Sexuality News of the Day

Question

What is happening in the news today that is related to human sexuality, and how do we know it's true? How does a news event relate to us and our values and choices?

General Objective

Students will learn what is being talked about in the news and will find out how to use medically accurate sources to check facts.

Measurable Objective

Students will be able to talk about one current event that is related to sexuality and give a reliable, medically accurate source for the information.

When a Person Says He or She Is Transgender

Information from Central Toronto Youth Services

It's hard to hear that a person isn't who you thought he or she was. It may take some time to get your head around it. Yet experts who work with transgender people say:

1. **This person is not alone.** Although there are no solid statistics, researchers estimate 1 in 1,000 people are born each year feeling that the gender of his or her body (how it looks on the outside) and spirit (how he or she feels on the inside) are different.

2. **Being transgender is not the same as being gay.** *Sexual orientation* and *sexual identity* are terms used to describe who we are attracted to and who we love romantically. *Heterosexual, gay, lesbian,* and *bisexual* are words you are probably familiar with. We all have a sexual orientation. We all also have a gender identity—the inner feeling that we are a man or a woman, that we are masculine or feminine, or perhaps somewhere on a "continuum" between masculine and feminine. Being transgender is about gender identity. For trans people, their bodies do not match their inner experience of gender.

3. **Parents don't "make" a child trans.** It's not clear why some people are transgender, but there is no evidence that socialization or parenting either causes or can prevent it. Gender identity is just part of one's core identity. This person has been brave enough and honest enough to embark on this scary and necessary process—and trusts people around him or her enough to tell them about what's happening to him or her. Be supportive of the entire family.

4. **The transgender person is taking important steps toward being happier and healthier by coming out.** You may not notice it right away, but as time passes you will see the transgender person become happier, more comfortable, more at ease. The serious distress many transgender people feel about their bodies begins to resolve itself during transition. Transitioning can include both social and physical changes—like a name change, a change in clothing or hairstyle, hormones, or surgery. People transitioning from female to male (FTM) are trans boys/men, or just boys/men, and should be referred to using male pronouns, and vice versa with people transitioning from male to female (MTF).

5. **Know that the world isn't going to end.** Life goes on. You and the transgender person will find that a lot of life continues the same. While some people may be judgmental, you will also find support in unexpected places. There is acceptance in the world that you might not have known about before.

This handout may be reproduced for educational, noncommercial uses only (with this copyright line). From *Healthy Teen Relationships: Using Values and Choices to Teach Sex Education* by Martha R. Roper. Copyright © 2011 by Search Institute®, Minneapolis, Minnesota, 877-240-7251 ext. 1, www.search-institute.org. All rights reserved. Adapted from *Families in TRANSition: A Resource Guide for Parents of Trans Youth*, with permission from Central Toronto Youth Services. www.ctys.org/programs/prideprejudiceparents.htm.

Time and Materials

- 10 to 15 minutes

A computer with Internet access and/or a news source to hold up and read to students. **Note:** If you want to use the news as a daily activity, you may bring the same source or a variety of sources. If you want to expose students to one big lesson on news sources, bring enough printed news articles so that each student may have one for the group activity. Also include a few faux news articles, "advertorials," or ads disguised as a news article (usually found in magazines or newspapers).

Instructions

Tell the students that while they are taking a sex education class, current events are still relevant to our studies. Ask them where they get their daily news, and ask how they know that something is true. They may have no news sources, or many; there may be a high level of sophistication among news sources or not.

REAL THOUGHTS FROM TEENS

"What does Viagra do to a woman if she takes it? How about a teenage boy?"

Show students a current story from a newspaper, magazine, or online news site. (If you have a projector or an interactive whiteboard, online news is better, because most students get news online more than anywhere else.) Give students a complete citation of your article. You may read the first few paragraphs or invite a student to read to the class. Make sure it is an interesting topic and that you have checked out whether the story is true. Have a couple of articles ready to go if their interest fades. Ask them: "How do we find out if what we read is true? How have your teachers taught you to look up whether the writer is giving you opinions or facts?" Let students tell the class how they find out whether something is true. Someone will say he uses Google and someone will say she uses Wikipedia, and someone will say something that you have not heard before. Tell students they can find out for certain whether something is true, but it requires looking in several places. Explain that Google and Wikipedia may point them to the right direction to find the truth, but they may also have to wade through some misinformation to get there. Google search results aren't scrutinized for their accuracy, and Wikipedia articles can be edited by anyone unless locked, but within those Google results are useful sources, and at the end of each Wikipedia entry is usually a reference list that links to some great primary sources. A primary source should be the original document or idea.

Hold up a newspaper or printed page that looks like an article but is really an advertisement. Start reading from the top and see if you get any reaction from the students. Ask if this article sounds true, and why it does or doesn't. Ask if they wonder who wrote this and why. Show them that it's an advertisement that is supposed to look like an article.

Now give each student an article to skim. Ask him to read it for a feel about whether it is factual or not, and to look for who wrote and published the article, so that he can turn to the next student and tell her the content and the citation.

Ask each student to turn to the person next to him and share his article and the citation. Ask the students to guess what is true and what isn't and why. Invite the students to share their articles with the larger group and tell them whether they think it's true and why.

Give the students a list of sources for medically accurate websites for general health and sexuality information and websites intended to educate adolescents, found in the back of this book under "resources." You might also want to include websites such as:

- The *New York Times* (nytimes.com)
- *USA Today* (usatoday.com)
- The *Wall Street Journal* (wsj.com)
- *Time* magazine (time.com)
- *Newsweek* (newsweek.com)
- CNN (cnn.com)
- NPR (npr.org)
- The BBC (bbc.co.uk)
- The home pages of Yahoo!, MSN, and Google
- The home page of your local newspaper
- The home page of your school newspaper
- The school website

Make sure that you take the time to walk through at least one website, such as medlineplus.gov.

Notes

The chapter on values in Deborah Roffman's *Sex & Sensibility: The Thinking Parent's Guide to Talking Sense About Sex* (Boston: Perseus Publishing, 2001) was very helpful; she explained how she talks to students and parents about values being a summation of attitudes and feelings that are important to decision making. She says that we constantly make microdecisions based on what we value. Therefore, when talking with adolescents about values, it is their job to formulate their own values and behave accordingly. Any pressure we put on them to do exactly *what* we want *when* we want them to do it is heard with defiance and is therefore not helpful to them in finding their own way. Listening to kids and really sympathizing with them and expressing our own opinions as simply that is more positive than telling them what to believe, value, and do. The beauty of the classroom with a skilled teacher is that young people can exchange ideas in a safe place where they are allowed to own their opinions and share why they believe what they do. Everyone in the room is allowed to believe what they want and share it in a classroom. That said, one cannot make up one's own facts and expect to not be challenged.

When opinions are based on religious teachings, there is an exception because those beliefs are not necessarily based on facts. If I, the teacher, am the only one in the room who is offended by an opinion expressed that is based on a religious belief, I will go ahead and say that I am offended and why. Each person is allowed to do this. At some point the teacher has to make an executive decision to move on—to agree to disagree. I usually end by saying: "And that's why I love America. We get to hold differing opinions."

Dress Codes and Body Art

Question

What do your clothing choices and your body art say about you? Why do schools get to make rules about what you wear to school and how you look?

General Objective

Students will understand that their clothing choices and their body art send a message about who they are.

Measurable Objective

Students will create a list of five personal dos and don'ts that they want to practice to be true to the personal messages they want to send about themselves.

Time and Materials

- 45 to 90 minutes
- A local school dress code to share as a handout to the class.
- Images of a variety of clothing styles, some of which are revealing and against school dress codes. Put the images in a box or prepare a PowerPoint presentation. Make sure to include items found in popular clothing stores that "push the boundaries": T-shirts and sweatpants with suggestive writing, low-cut pants, short shorts, revealing or suggestive outfits for young children. You may want to collect actual clothing items and bring them in on hangers, but make sure to clear it with your school or program administrator first.
- Paper and markers

Instructions

Invite students to generate a list of dress code rules at their school and write them on easel paper. Many may not know there are rules. State that there are often disagreements among adults as to whether a top is too low or whether an adult should even look to see whether a top is too low or pants are too low. Adults are concerned about being accused of noticing too much.

> **REAL THOUGHTS FROM TEENS**
> "Talk about boys who insist sex isn't that big of a deal."

Pass out the school dress code from a local school or have students open their own school handbook and find the dress code. Ask what their reactions are. State again that students are allowed to hold their own opinions, but they may not create their own facts.

Talk about how clothing and body art are portrayed in the media, particularly in things that are marketed toward teens. This is an opportunity to bring up students' assumptions in a respectful way. For example, do males generally want to see more skin? Do they find the exposure distracting when they are trying to concentrate? Should students who feel distracted go to single-sex schools? Should parents be required to buy new clothes for students who have a closet full of clothes that are not appropriate for school?

Divide students into small groups and have them make up their own school dress code, consisting of five dos and five don'ts. After five minutes, have students report their lists to the entire class. Help them consolidate their lists into one master list of five dos and five don'ts intended for their school principal.

Next, hand out paper and markers and ask students to draw a T-shirt slogan that states their philosophy for the day. Tell the students that their message to the world has to be socially acceptable and comply with the school dress code.

After several minutes, go around the room and have each person answer the following questions:

"Why did you choose this?"
"What do you think the slogan means?"
"Does this slogan have double meanings?"
"How would you edit this slogan to better represent yourself?"

Notes

If you have a dress code, you might share that with students. For example: "The Board of Education and (the teachers) agrees that teachers should project a professional image in dress, language, and conduct. During the school day and at school-related activities, teachers should model professional conduct that sets an example for students."

Tell them how you feel about the code and whether you agree or respectfully disagree with a word, phrase, or idea. Tell them that it is your choice to comply because you want to work in this organization and be seen as a person who is professional, which means projecting a professional look.

Definition of Abstinence Education according to the U.S. Government[1]

Abstinence education refers to an educational or motivational program that:

   A. has as its exclusive purpose, teaching the social, psychological, and health gains to be realized by abstaining from sexual activity;

   B. teaches abstinence from sexual activity outside marriage as the expected standard for all school-age children;

   C. teaches that abstinence from sexual activity is the only certain way to avoid out-of-wedlock pregnancy, sexually transmitted diseases, and other associated health problems;

   D. teaches that a mutually faithful monogamous relationship in the context of marriage is the expected standard of human sexual activity;

E. teaches that sexual activity outside of the context of marriage is likely to have harmful psychological and physical effects;

F. teaches that bearing children out of wedlock is likely to have harmful consequences for the child, the child's parents, and society;

G. teaches young people how to reject sexual advances and how alcohol and drug use increases vulnerability to sexual advances; and

H. teaches the importance of attaining self-sufficiency before engaging in sexual activity.

A Is for Abstinence

Question

What is abstinence and how does it work?

General Objective

Students will have a clear sense of what abstinence means to them and will learn ways to say no to sexual pressure. They will also understand that if they do not choose abstinence, they must make smart choices about contraception and STI prevention.

Measurable Objective

Students will write answers to lines they may hear. They will write a personal belief statement about what abstinence means to them.

Time and Materials

- 45 minutes
- One die
- Easel pad or whiteboard

Instructions

Ask students what they think *abstinence* means. Generally, you'll find that there is an agreement that it means to not have sexual intercourse. Ask them to consider that there is a continuum of sexual behavior, and that we need to define our terms really clearly so that not only we in this room know what we are talking about but also because we will want to be able to talk with our partners and healthcare providers using the correct vocabulary.

One main idea to tell students about abstinence is that it can be a philosophy, or a religious belief, a personal value, or simply a method of birth control. Students often hear "Abstinence works 100 percent of the time." While it is true that the method of abstinence for birth control is 100 percent effective, that's true *only if students are abstinent 100 percent of the time.*

Tell students that everyone needs to learn *how* to abstain when they want to abstain from sexual intercourse. Some times they might want to abstain are:

1. On a first date, on a second date, when they are not yet engaged, when they are not married. . . . Encourage the students to have a conversation about the pros and cons of having intercourse early in a relationship.
2. If they have never had intercourse before.
3. If their religious beliefs dictate no sex before marriage.
4. If they have been drinking or using drugs or taking prescription medication.
5. If they're at a party and don't know anyone that well.
6. If they don't have a solid relationship with the person.
7. If they don't have protection.
8. If the person used to date their best friend.
9. If they don't have privacy.
10. If the other person has been drinking or using drugs.
11. If they don't want to for any reason.
12. If they don't want to worry about pregnancy or becoming a teenage parent.
13. If they don't know about the morning-after pill or how to get it.
14. If they are afraid the person will break their heart.
15. If they don't understand anything about sexual pleasure, sexual body parts, or what makes a great sexual experience between two people.
16. If they don't feel comfortable or interested in having a conversation with that person about anything concerning the topic of sex.
17. If they were absent from school the day the teacher talked about how to abstain or use birth control.
18. If they don't understand the risks involved.
19. If they have promised themselves they won't have sex until _____.
20. _____
21. _____

Everyone can add to the list. Any person may pass.

Now take the die and hold it up to the students. Tell them that using the method of abstinence to prevent pregnancy, sexually transmitted diseases, and negative sexual situations is 100 percent effective, *but only if they use it 100 percent of the time, no exceptions.* If they decide to have sex but don't use protection, they are taking a big risk: they're rolling the dice for themselves and their partners. Roll the die and show that, for example, if 1 comes up, nothing bad happens. Roll again, and say there is a pregnancy. Roll again and there is the human papillomavirus (HPV) and genital warts. Roll again and there is chlamydia. Keep rolling the die and adding different negative consequences, including getting pregnant and contracting HIV in one night.

Have students get into groups and make a list of ways to say no to intercourse. Then have students make a big list on the easel pad or whiteboard. Someone can type the list in a word processing software document and bring it to class next time, or a student can write it onto an interactive whiteboard and make copies after the list is made.

Get back into groups and ask students to list what else they can do besides intercourse, from going for a walk together all the way to more personal and intimate sexual behaviors. (*Outercourse* is the word used for hugs and kisses and anything that does not involve penetration.) Make sure the list is no/low risk for pregnancy and STIs.

REAL THOUGHTS FROM TEENS

"**Many kids are too afraid that their partner will break up with them because they don't want to have sex, so they have sex even though they don't want to.**"

Notes

Students may want to have a deep conversation about abstinence for any number of reasons. The reasons to stop the conversation include running out of time, if someone is talking too much and not listening to others, or if someone gets too personal or silly. The topic of virginity and what it means to be a virgin is personal and sometimes religious. I tell students that if someone asks them if they are a virgin, they should say: "Why do you want to know?" This question can be said in many ways depending on which word is emphasized, what your tone of voice is like, and how you intend the person to feel as you say it. You can say "Why do you want to know?" and honestly want to know the answer, or you can say it with righteous indignation. If you want to continue the relationship, you can say it with honest curiosity, and then be quiet and listen. The short answer for ending the relationship is "That's none of your business." Either reply depends on the way it's said, the intention of the speaker, and the way the conversation goes from there.

Exploring the Options

Question

What are the choices when a pregnancy happens?

General Objective

Students will understand that there are several choices after unprotected intercourse.

Measurable Objective

Each student will list the choices after unprotected intercourse and write a short personal reflection showing their values and choices.

Time and Materials

- 45 to 90 minutes

Instructions

State law may require that any school with a sex education program must include the topics of adoption, parenting, Plan B, the abortion pill, and the abortion procedure. It is important to review the current state laws on access to emergency contraception, the abortion pill, and the abortion procedure.

There is usually a card in the Question Box that says something along the lines of: "How can I have sex and not use protection, but not get pregnant or infected with a disease?"

Begin by pulling that question out of the box (even if you have to write it yourself). Read the question, and then say: "You can't." Read the question again and answer it again. Tell the students that if they are not able to protect themselves from pregnancy and infection, then they are not ready to have sex. That said, many teens have sex anyway, and 10 percent of girls who have sex get pregnant. Therefore, they'll need to go over the options that teens have when abstinence fails.

Review the choices available after a person has unprotected intercourse. Show a diagram with the choices, or write them on easel paper, and introduce each choice with a brief explanation, including the state laws about age of access to abortion and adoption services.

Then have each student choose an option and list the pros and cons of the option. Ask students to not use "fighting words" like *kill* and *murder* when talking about abortion because each person decides for himself what his opinion is on these sensitive topics.

Each group will report to the class about what they see as the pros and cons of each choice. After all groups have reported, there can be some careful conversation and discussion about the topic. Each group should be reminded that they are allowed to disagree and agree to disagree about important topics.

Notes

Teachers may take several classes for this discussion, or move through the activity and cover the subject fairly quickly. Be ready for questions and comments about religion, ethics, morals, and right and wrong to surface in the discussions. Continue to state that everyone has a right to their own opinion, but that said, we may not make things up and state them as facts to support our opinions. Students may explain what their personal faith is and how it impacts their belief. They are expected to "agree to disagree" about their beliefs.

Boys in the class tend to have ambivalent feelings about how they experience this lesson, since they have no legal right to know about or decide what will happen with the pregnancy. I tell them from the beginning of the lesson that this is the case and that if they care about what happens to their pregnancy, then they need to pay attention to planning parenthood. In other words: abstain or use the correct condom, correctly, and consistently.

Endnote
1. U.S. Social Security Act, § 510(b)(2) (codified at 42 U.S.C. § 710(b)(2)).

Chapter 5

Strengthening Sexual Communication Skills

This chapter contains activities designed to help students develop their communication skills through role play and discussion. "Communicating Sexual Choices" encourages students to think about their choices and then communicate them clearly to another person, while "Refusal Lines" lets them practice resistance skills. If and when students decide to have sex, "The ABCs of Sex" teaches them how to have a discussion about contraception and safer sex with a partner. "Sexuality in Cyberspace" addresses the many issues involved with online sexual communication, while "Difficult Conversations" lets students practice talking with a parent, guardian, or trusted adult about an unplanned pregnancy.

REAL THOUGHTS FROM TEENS

"Who do you go to when there's a problem or you're scared?"

Communicating Sexual Choices

Question

What does it mean to talk and communicate effectively about sexuality?

General Objectives

Students will learn a variety of ways to effectively communicate how they feel about sexuality and their sexual choices.

Students will be reminded to tell the truth and say "I" messages: "When _____, I feel _____ because I think _____. I would like _____."

Students will learn to consider whether they want a relationship to be sexual or not.

Students will learn to say no and practice saying no with their body language, clothing style, word choices, conversation style, and clear repetition of words and actions to end the conversation.

Measurable Objective

Students will demonstrate to the class that they know how to use the "I" message correctly and effectively in a roleplay situation.

Time and Materials

- 45 to 90 minutes
- Easel paper and markers
- Magazine fashion photos, advertising photos, video clips that show different styles of body language, clothing choices, word choices, and conversation styles with clear communication

- Photo of young people drinking and partying and a photo of young people having fun not drinking
- Barbie, Ken, and Skipper or any other appropriate dolls to make the point of older male and younger female
- Sexual Decision Making Chart—one blank and one filled out (see pages 72–73)
- Sexual Communication Skills handout (see page 75) for observers of the demonstration skits
- Printouts of the Centers for Disease Control's latest Youth Risk Behavior Survey (available at cdc.gov/HealthyYouth/yrbs/pdf/us_sexual_trend_yrbs.pdf)

Instructions

Tell students that they have choices about their sexual behavior. They can choose (1) complete abstinence or shades of abstinence, (2) sexual behavior with protection from pregnancy and sexually transmitted infections and HIV/AIDS, or (3) they can choose to participate in dangerous sexual activity with no protection, which puts them and their partners at high risk.

Tell students that in order to control what they want to happen in their sexual story or life history, they must first know what they want among the choices available at that particular time. Then they must know how to communicate that effectively. Finally, they need to actually use the skills they have learned in real-life situations. Learning and practicing sexual communication and conflict management skills such as the ones taught here will make it more likely that students will use the skills when they need to.

Tell students that the point of these lessons on sexual communication is to teach them how to resist pressure to have sexual intercourse, or at least resist having sex in an unsafe or dangerous way. Everyone can benefit from learning and using effective communication skills. They are the basis of healthy teen relationships and help kids make safe sexual decisions. Remind them that more than half of students in high school choose to not have sexual intercourse, and then hand them the printout from the CDC's Youth Risk Behavior Survey.[1]

Now write on the easel paper the heading "Effective Sexual Communication Skills," and explain that it's possible to tell a lot from the way people dress, communicate, and behave. Write down "Body Language" and show magazine ads or video clips of young people interacting. Ask students: "What do you think the person is trying to communicate?" Then write "Clothing Style" and show ads for clothing. Follow with "Word Choices/'I' Messages and Conversation Style" and show a video clip that portrays young people using a style of language that is disrespectful or too casual about sexual behavior. And finally write down "Clear Communication with Words" and show video clips that depict negative and positive communication.

Have a discussion about the students' reactions to and assumptions about what they've seen. Ask them: "How would you communicate that you are choosing abstinence or some kind of sex?"

Now look at this blank map of your sexual decisions. It shows where you continue to come to a fork in the road and that you must continue to make choices. Here is the handout with the top chart blank and the bottom part of the chart filled out. I want you to sit for a couple of minutes and read the chart that is filled out. See if you can picture yourself communicating at every fork in the road. Explain what it means to be in safe or dangerous situations, and explain that people usually have more control over situations than they know. Stress, however, that forced sexual intercourse is just that—forced, and there is no blame on the victim for that. Even when a person is under the influence of alcohol or drugs, it does not mean they want to have some kind of sex or to be raped. Explain that decisions must be made and communicated in order to fully express their values and choices. They must think of it as a mental map.

REAL THOUGHTS FROM TEENS

"I was in a situation where I had sex with someone whom I wasn't engaged in a relationship with. We had met once or twice and I had walked to his house while his parents were gone and my parents didn't know. He didn't ask my consent, but I didn't object. Is that sexual assault or rape? What if I don't consider it either of those?"

Beach Story Lesson

At this point, get out Barbie, Ken, and Barbie's little sister, Skipper. Tell the class the following story:

Barbie doesn't want to go to the beach house with her parents and little sister this year because she's 21 and feels too old. She wants to stay home with her friends. Skipper, 13 years old, goes with their parents, and before she walks out to the beach alone on Monday morning, her parents tell her three rules: Stay in our sight from our deck. Call us with your cell and ask for permission if you want to go somewhere. Last, do not walk away with strangers.

Ken, 21, walks up to Skipper and asks to talk. Ken explains that he is waiting for his friends to join him at the beach for the week. His parents are not going to be there because he is old enough to stay alone. Ken and Skipper talk, and he asks her how old she is. She says she's 17. He invites her to go up to his deck for a drink. She goes and does not call her parents to tell them she is leaving the beach. She goes into Ken's house, tours the house, and has a drink with alcohol. She gets into his hot tub, and then she gets dizzy from the drink and can't remember what else happens.

Ask the class to discuss Skipper's and Ken's decisions by looking at the easel paper. Write the concerns the students have about their decisions:

Ken probably knew Skipper was too young for him. He knew she was too young to drink. Because Skipper claimed to be 17, Ken put himself in legal jeopardy for statutory rape and—because Skipper was actually under the age of 14—child sexual abuse. Ken probably knew that he was seducing her and putting them both in a dangerous sexual situation.

Skipper lied about her age. She broke all three rules of her parents. She went into a house alone with a man 21 or older while she was just 13. Skipper put herself in a potentially dangerous situation by drinking and getting into a hot tub. She could have drowned, and she could have been raped. She was definitely in trouble with her parents. She lost their trust.

Sexual Decision Making
by Heather Corrina of www.scarleteen.com (adapted by permission)

When we're figuring out if we're ready for sex with a partner, if we want to ask ourselves the most basic questions possible, those are:

- Do I want to have this kind/these kinds of sex for myself, physically, emotionally, and intellectually? Do the other person's physical, emotional, and intellectual wants also seem in alignment?
- Do I want to do this at this time, in this setting, with this particular person? Does the other person want to do what we're going to now and with me?
- Do I have a good sense of what possible wanted and unwanted experiences and outcomes this can entail? Do I feel pretty prepared for them? How about the person I'm about to have sex with: is he or she aware and prepared?

- If there are unwanted outcomes I can avoid—like pregnancy, infection, getting hurt in some way—am I prepared with what I need to do/use to try and prevent them? Is the other person? Are we in agreement about the ways we're going to protect ourselves?
- Do I feel really good about the answers to those four questions?

If you said yes to the last question, then you and your partner(s) are probably in a sound position to have a kind of sex together and more likely to have positive outcomes. If you said no to the last question, then one or both of you might want to press pause and rethink your choices and/or take some time to make changes to whatever needs changing to get you both to that yes.

SEXUAL DECISION MAKING CHART

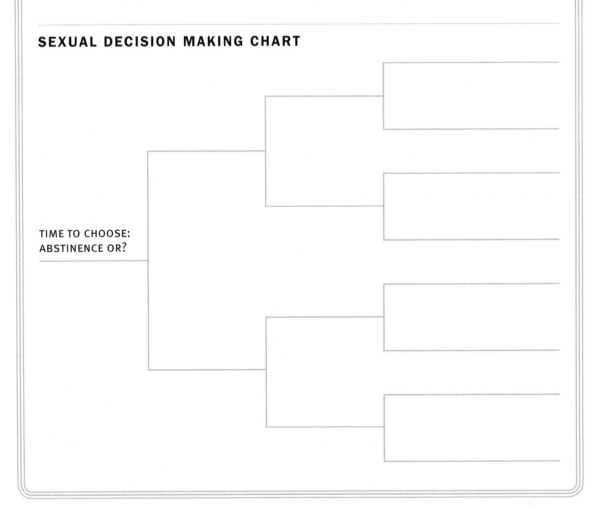

TIME TO CHOOSE:
ABSTINENCE OR?

SEXUAL DECISION MAKING CHART

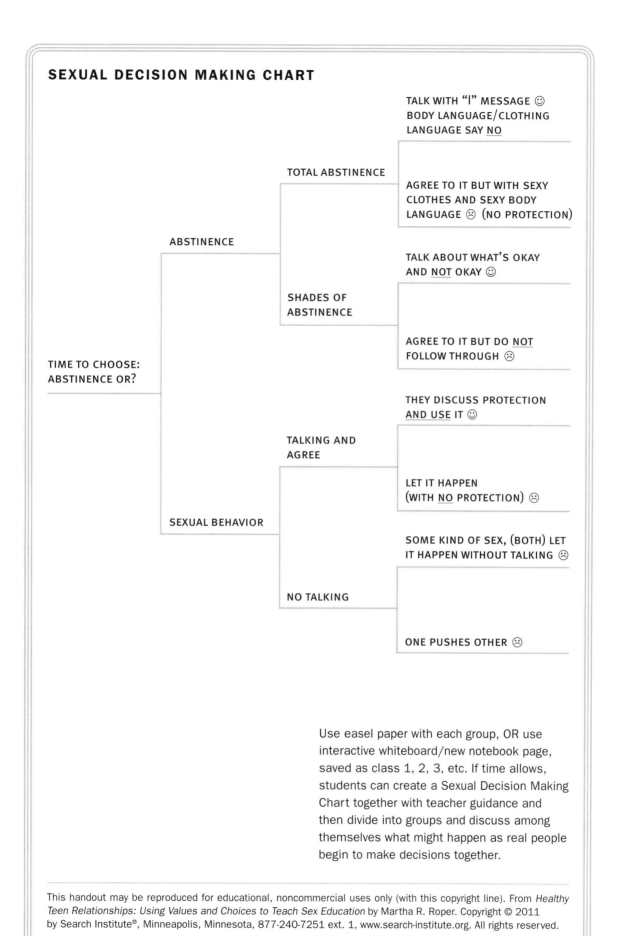

Use easel paper with each group, OR use interactive whiteboard/new notebook page, saved as class 1, 2, 3, etc. If time allows, students can create a Sexual Decision Making Chart together with teacher guidance and then divide into groups and discuss among themselves what might happen as real people begin to make decisions together.

This handout may be reproduced for educational, noncommercial uses only (with this copyright line). From *Healthy Teen Relationships: Using Values and Choices to Teach Sex Education* by Martha R. Roper. Copyright © 2011 by Search Institute®, Minneapolis, Minnesota, 877-240-7251 ext. 1, www.search-institute.org. All rights reserved.

Now let the students list problems that Skipper and Ken could have to deal with as a result of their sexual choices. For example: pregnancy; disease; rape; Skipper's parents charge Ken with child sexual abuse, resulting in him having a lifetime felony record of sex offender.

Ask students to get into small groups and create a list of dos and don'ts for what they feel is appropriate to clearly communicate their sexual choice to abstain from sexual intercourse. Ask groups to list suggestions for how students might improve their relationship skills from the very beginning. The point of learning and using effective communication skills is to know how to tell the truth and say what you think, feel, and want in any given sexual situation.

Give each student a Sexual Communication Skills sheet (see page 75). Give a brief explanation of what these mean and then divide students into small groups. Assign each group to take one of the skills and make a list of dos and don'ts to help their classmates understand the skill. Tell them they will be asked to share the list of dos and don'ts.

Before the groups give their short do's and don'ts of sexual communication report, ask all students to make some notes to share with the group during discussion time. If time allows, ask students to take the sample conversation starters and do some role plays using the new skills. Explain that they are allowed to help each other since these skills may be new.

After all the groups have reported, ask a couple of students to volunteer to show effective and ineffective ways to meet and start a conversation. Hand out a skills sheet and ask students to put a check beside the skill they observed in the demonstration. The student who is supposed to show us the skills may have a checklist, too, to guarantee some success.

Sample conversation starters:

"You would if you loved me."
"Everyone is doing it."
"I just want to feel close to you."
"Trust me. Don't be scared."
"You want me. I know you do."
"Want to get high? It will relax you."
"We've been going out for six months."
"You did it last weekend."

Refusal Lines

Elizabeth Casparian, Ph.D., and Eva Goldfarb, Ph.D., authors

Question

How can teens effectively communicate their choices?

Sexual Communication Skills

_____ Telling the Truth About Name, Age, School, But NOT Telling too Much

_____ Body Language Clearly Saying No

_____ Clothing Style with No Mixed Messages

_____ Word Choices/ I Messages
(I think _____,
I feel _____,
and I would like _____.)

_____ Conversation Style Friendly but Not Sexual

_____ Saying No and Repeating No

_____ Ending a Conversation Quickly and Confidently

This handout may be reproduced for educational, noncommercial uses only (with this copyright line). From _Healthy Teen Relationships: Using Values and Choices to Teach Sex Education_ by Martha R. Roper. Copyright © 2011 by Search Institute®, Minneapolis, Minnesota, 877-240-7251 ext. 1, www.search-institute.org. All rights reserved.

General Objective

Students will develop possible responses to pressure lines they might encounter in sexual situations and rehearse refusal skills to sexual pressure.

Measurable Objective

Students will write a list of five pressure lines and appropriate refusal lines.

Materials

- Pens or pencils
- Six copies of the Pressure Lines, Refusal Skills handout

Instructions

Answer, a national sex education advocacy group, has a great website that gives teachers training, resources, and lesson plans (answer.rutgers.edu). For example, here is their lesson on how to handle sexual lines that teens might hear. Practicing the responses in class by using this lesson is key to reinforcing the values and choices of sexual restraint that we hope young people will practice.

> **REAL THOUGHTS FROM TEENS**
>
> **"Is there a bad effect on you when you get older if you do different types of sexual stuff?"**

Explain to participants that one of the many aspects of teaching about abstinence is effective communication about sexual behavior. Young people may choose to abstain and really feel motivated to abstain, but without practicing how they will negotiate for abstinence, it is going to be difficult for many of them to follow through with this decision. This activity provides a unique opportunity for people to begin developing a vocabulary for how to talk with a partner about limits and boundaries that will help them abstain from risky sexual behavior.

Divide the class into groups of three or four. Instruct the small groups to assign a recorder for each group and give that person a pencil or pen. Explain to participants that in this activity, each small group will be given a sheet of paper that has a short scenario written on it about two people trying to negotiate a potential sexual situation. You will give each group the first line of dialogue, and they are to work together to create the next line in the dialogue. Then they are to pass their sheet on to the next group. Each group will create the next line of dialogue for the sheet they receive until the sheets get back to their original groups. Then the original group will read their sheets aloud. In every scenario, Partner A is pressuring and Partner B is refusing that pressure.

Give a handout to each group, and as you do so, read them one of the following lines of dialogue and have the group recorder write it down next to "Partner A":

- I know you want me as much as I want you.
- I've done so much for you. It's time you did something for me.
- Look—if you can't meet my needs, I'm going to find someone who can.
- I can't help myself—you're driving me crazy with the way you look at me and touch me. You've been asking for it all night!

- I know you had sex with someone else. Why don't you want to do it with me?
- I just want to make you feel good. What's the risk of one time?
- We've already had oral sex, so what's the big deal?
- If you really loved me, you'd do this with me.
- I know you've already had sex with other people. Why are you saying no now? It's not like you're a virgin anymore.
- Why don't you want to go down on me? You're supposed to know how to please your man/woman.
- I thought you were grown up—but you don't want to do this? You're just a kid.
- Don't you want to have a baby? Then we'll always be together.

Give the groups about three minutes to develop their response to this line and write it down next to "Partner B." Then have them pass the worksheet one group to the right or left, keeping this consistent throughout the activity. You will need to give them more time each time the sheet gets passed, because they will have to read the sheets before they can create a new line of dialogue.

When the sheets have been returned to their original group, have two group members read the entire dialogue to the class. After each sheet is read, ask the participants to discuss what they thought was more or less effective about how the "refuser" responded to each pressure line in the dialogue. Ask them how realistic the lines sounded. Go around until each group has had a chance to read their dialogue to the entire group.

Notes

Building on this lesson about how to respond to sexual lines, I like to have students get into groups and create a skit to present to the class that shows how a person can say, "Yes, I want to be closer, but I want to be safe." Each group can be told ahead of time to promote the use of condoms, oral contraceptives, or injectables, or to talk about visiting a local teen health center or Planned Parenthood so their questions can be answered, and methods of infection, disease, and pregnancy prevention can be obtained if they are not planning to abstain from intercourse.

The ABCs of Sex

Question

How do teens start a discussion with partners about contraception?

General Objective

Students will learn to talk effectively about contraception with their potential partners.

Measurable Objective

Students will get a positive evaluation from their group in demonstrating effective communication about the use of abstinence, birth control, or condoms.

Pressure Lines, Refusal Skills

Partner A wants to have sex, Partner B does not want to risk pregnancy or disease in any way and does not want to have sex. Work with your group to come up with an effective next line in this dialogue and then pass the sheet to the next group.

PLEASE WRITE CLEARLY SO OTHERS CAN READ YOUR HANDWRITING!

Partner A:

Partner B:

Partner A:

Partner B:

Partner A:

Partner B:

This handout may be reproduced for educational, noncommercial uses only (with this copyright line). From *Healthy Teen Relationships: Using Values and Choices to Teach Sex Education* by Martha R. Roper. Copyright © 2011 by Search Institute®, Minneapolis, Minnesota, 877-240-7251 ext. 1, www.search-institute.org. All rights reserved. Copyright © 2007, Answer, Rutgers University. All Rights Reserved.

Time and Materials
- 30 to 45 minutes
- Easel paper and tape

Instructions

First, introduce two new sets of skills on sheets of easel paper:

Sexual Restraint Skills

Wear clothing that says no.

Have a facial expression that says no.

Move your body in ways that say no.

If you want to leave the situation, turn around and leave. Use a cell phone.

Say "I" messages: "When ___, I feel ____ because I think _____. I would like ____."

Try to keep the relationship if you want to and suggest doing something else.

Defend yourself against verbal and/or physical attack.

Ask for help from others.

Dial for help: parents or other trusted adult and/or 911

Skills for Having a Conversation about Using Protection

Use "I" messages: "When ___, I feel ____ because I think _____. I would like ____."

If you agree, say so.

If you don't agree, say so and state why.

Come to an understanding and confirm what you just said.

Ask if the other person feels okay.

If yes, proceed with plan.

If no, listen and start over.

Then ask students to get into groups of three. Each person will choose to be person A, B, or C. The person who chose A will practice talking about abstinence. The person who chose B will practice talking about the birth control pill, and the person who chose C will practice talking about the condom. One person will try to get the other to agree to sexual activity. Each person will take turns rotating out of the conversation in order to observe how the role play went, taking notes, and giving feedback to the others about whether they did or did not say what they wanted to do and make plans to do that.

After a few minutes, one group can volunteer to share their role play in front of the class. Ask students: "Did the subject of infection come up in your conversations, or just pregnancy or other reason to have sex or not to have sex? What were the reasons? Did the subject of infection come up as a reason to use protection or not to use protection? Discuss." The person who did the observing will want to refer to notes to share observations. Role playing and talking about it takes practice, so plan to teach and reteach the skills

> **REAL THOUGHTS FROM TEENS**
> "Can taking pills to get rid of a baby hurt you?"

so the students will get used to observing and stating what they observed and making a thoughtful comment about it.

Then ask students to get back into their ABC group of three people, but this time change roles from A to B and B to C and C to A. This time when they start the role play each person makes the point that they are concerned about getting a sexually transmitted infection. Let the role plays go on and then ask again for students to make their observations about what happened.

Have the students share their observations while you write the results on easel paper. Let this happen several times to review the importance of knowing your values and using good choices with your language and your behavior.

Notes

This lesson is so important that you may want to stretch it out over two class periods. It is important to use the skills for communication and conflict management at every opportunity in the classroom so students will see how they work in normal daily life.

Sexuality in Cyberspace

Question

What do we need to know about citizenship in cyberspace?

General Objective

Students need to learn basic communication skills for navigating through texting, social networking, and being online as well as how to identify bullying and threats. They need to make a commitment to use social media respectfully.

Measurable Objective

Students will write a personal commitment plan that will pledge that the student will not join in cyberbullying or sexting.

Time and Materials

- 45 minutes
- A 3" x 5" index card for each student

Instructions

Ask students how old they were when they got their first e-mail address. How many have laptops that they use in the privacy of their bedrooms? How old were they when they got their first cell phones? (If someone doesn't have a cell phone, encourage him to explain why.) How many are on a social networking site, and how much time do they spend there? Take this opportunity to remind students that electronic communications (including e-mails, browsing history, pictures, and text messages) leave a record that is very difficult to remove; even if they erase the material from their

REAL THOUGHTS FROM TEENS
"What are your thoughts on abortion?"

own phones and computers, others—including their Internet provider or cell phone company—may not.

Allow students to get together in small groups and create a role play about texting or instant messaging (IM). They may get out their own cell phones and sit back to back, but they must only pretend to text or instant message and say their words out loud. Each role play must create a difficult situation in which a person gets out of trouble in an appropriate way.

Possible Role Play Topics
- Someone asks you out in a text or IM.
- Someone says "I love you" for the first time in a text or IM.
- You receive a text or IM from someone who has been flirting with you, only it's intended for someone else.
- You receive a text or IM from a new boyfriend or girlfriend wanting to know why your online profile status reads "single."
- You receive a text or IM that addresses you as "Honey" or "Baby" and you don't want to be called that.
- Your new partner wants to know who you've been dating.
- Your new partner wants to know whether you're a virgin.
- You receive a text or IM that is way too sexual for you.
- Your new partner wants to know what you're wearing.
- Your new partner wants you to send a photo of what you're wearing.
- Your new partner wants you to text sexual words.
- Your new partner breaks up with you in a text or IM.
- You get a text at a party from a friend who says your angry ex is on the way in to find you.

Ask students to write on an index card what they would require of others in a relationship, and ask for a commitment to treat others the same way they want to be treated. They can hand in the cards to be read now, or you can share their wisdom during the next class.

Difficult Conversations
Martha R. Roper and Dr. Erin Keegan

Question
How do people react when they learn of an unplanned pregnancy?

General Objective
Young people will be able to observe, feel, and discuss the various experiences of family members as they try to solve the problems that an unplanned teen pregnancy causes.

Measurable Objective

Students will write five "I learned . . ." or "I am reminded . . ." statements about the complications of an unplanned teen pregnancy.

Time and Materials

- 45 to 90 minutes
- Character guide (see below)
- Easel paper and markers

Instructions

Briefly describe this situation to the class: A teenage girl is pregnant, and her mother has called a meeting with the boy and his parents to decide what to do. Explain to students that in real life, all the people involved would not likely come together for a formal sit-down to discuss what should happen.

Pass out copies of the handout of character descriptions, found below, and then divide the class into six groups, assigning each group a character. Have one member of each group read her or his character description aloud to the others, and then ask for a volunteer from each group to play the role. All other members of each group then become character advocates, providing coaching and support for the member playing the role. Ask role players to form a circle in the center and introduce themselves using the character description provided at the top of their page. Tell the support groups that they may not talk, but encourage them to write notes and pass them to their group member while the meeting is in progress.

REAL THOUGHTS FROM TEENS

"What are your feelings about abstinence?"

Tell role players to follow these rules:

1. Accept and adopt the facts of the role.
2. Become the role.
3. Experience the emotions involved in the role.
4. It is okay to change attitude(s) during the action.
5. Avoid consulting role notes during the role play.
6. Do not overact. It may detract from the learning goals.

Then, ask the person playing Jessica's mother to start the meeting by explaining why the meeting was called. Allow the meeting to proceed until there is a natural break.

After the first round of the role play, write "Norms for Difficult Conversations" on easel paper and list the following:

- Move from certainty to curiosity.
- Listen with the intent to understand and without resistance.
- Focus on issues, not personalities.
- Tell your truth quietly without blame or judgment.
- Be open to solutions, but not attached to your own.[2]

Character Guide

Jessica Stevenson: *Age 16, sheltered up-bringing, religious, close to family, 8-year-old brother, good student, junior in high school.*

You have been dating Tyler, age 17, a senior, for one year. When you met, you were immediately attracted to each other and wanted to have sex long before you finally did. You were hesitant to have intercourse because of your religious beliefs and family values, but the sexual attraction you felt for Tyler was so strong you gradually changed your mind.

Now that you are eight weeks pregnant, you feel shame and embarrassment. You think you were stupid to have sex, especially since you didn't even get that much pleasure out of it. You have felt guilty, and you never had an orgasm in the five times you had sex. You are angry with Tyler, but also love him and defend him to your parents.

You are confused and don't know what you want to do.

Tyler Williams: *Age 17, middle class upbringing, religious, close to family, two older brothers in college, good student, senior in high school.*

You have dated Jessica for one year. You like her a lot—maybe even love her—but you can't get too serious with anyone now because you plan to go away to college in a few months.

You do not share Jessica's religious beliefs, but you waited patiently for nine months until she agreed to sexual intercourse one night after a long session of private, intimate contact. The sex for you was great. She has felt guilty and said she didn't want to have sex again, but always changed her mind. You have had sex four other times with her since then. You didn't use contraception because Jessica said you didn't need to.

Now Jessica is eight weeks pregnant. You are sorry it happened and regret not using a condom or other contraception. You think she should get an abortion, but only if she wants to. You know you are not ready to be a parent right now.

Mrs. Williams: *Age 45, Tyler's mother, three sons (two in college), divorced Tyler's father five years ago, ex-husband remarried (tense relationship with him), public school teacher.*

You knew Tyler had a special girlfriend, Jessica, and are not surprised about your son's sexual activity or the girl's pregnancy. This same situation happened to your oldest son several years ago, and it was very hard on the family. You think Jessica should do what she wants, but you lean toward an abortion because you have no intention of paying for the baby's care. If they decide to keep the baby, Tyler will have to work to support his child, as you can't afford any major commitment. You want Tyler to go to college and would hate to see anything get in the way. You are still angry with your ex-husband and don't like him being in this conversation.

Mr. Williams: *Age 48, Tyler's father, divorced Tyler's mother five years ago and remarried, three sons from first marriage, not religious, salesman.*

You are prepared to speak up to defend Tyler because you feel this is Jessica's problem to resolve. What can you expect given the way teenage girls behave nowadays? Tyler may not even be the baby's father. Jessica knew what she was doing when she had unprotected sex and should take responsibility for her actions. You welcome the opportunity to stand up for Tyler because you feel guilty about leaving him five years ago. Nobody is going to hurt or take advantage of your son!

Mrs. Stevenson: *Age 38, Jessica's mother, two children, married 17 years, religious, against abortion, nurse.*

You are shocked and hurt that your daughter is pregnant. You thought she had better judgment than this and feel betrayed. You don't want a baby in the house and can envision getting stuck to help care for this one. You think your daughter was irresponsible and so was her boyfriend. You think the discussion of solutions is unnecessary. You are totally against abortion.

Mr. Stevenson: *Age 40, Jessica's father, married 17 years, two children, religious, engineer.*

You can't believe that this is happening to your baby girl. You thought it was cute that she had a serious boyfriend, until now. You blame Tyler—he took advantage of your dear, sweet, innocent daughter. You're upset to think that your wife will have another baby in the house to take care of because you and she are just beginning to enjoy each other again after getting your own children in school. Life was going so well until this happened.

This handout may be reproduced for educational, noncommercial uses only (with this copyright line). From *Healthy Teen Relationships: Using Values and Choices to Teach Sex Education* by Martha R. Roper. Copyright © 2011 by Search Institute®, Minneapolis, Minnesota, 877-240-7251 ext. 1, www.search-institute.org. All rights reserved.

If you also need to make a list of dos and don'ts with the group's help, then do that. At any point during the role play, anyone can call a time-out and add a communication or conflict management skill to the easel paper.

Then ask for different people to step into the roles, again allowing the rest of the groups to contribute notes to the new players. Continue this role play as long as the group can stay focused.

Note

You can write new character descriptions if you would like to role play a variety of situations.

Endnotes

1. U.S. Centers for Disease Control, *Trends in the Prevalence of Sexual Behaviors—National YRBS, 1991–2009*, Atlanta, GA: U.S. Centers for Disease Control and Prevention, Division of Adolescent and School Health, available at cdc.gov/HealthyYouth/yrbs/pdf/us_sexual_trend_yrbs.pdf, 2009.
2. Stone, Douglas, Bruce Patton, and Sheila Heen, *Difficult Conversations: How to Discuss What Matters Most*. New York: Penguin, 1999.

Books and Articles for Professionals

Teaching Sex Education

All Together Now: Teaching about Contraception and Safer Sex by Planned Parenthood Federations of America. New York: Planned Parenthood Federation of America, 2006

Bright Ideas: A Pocket Mentor For Beginning Teachers (6th ed.) by M. C. Clement. Washington, D.C.: National Education Association of the U.S., 2002.

Doing Gender Diversity: Readings in Theory and Real-World Experience by R. F. Plante and L. M. Maurer, Eds. Boulder, CO.: Westview Press, 2009.

Dude, You're a Fag: Masculinity and Sexuality in High School by C. J. Pascoe. Berkeley, CA: University of California Press, 2007.

Educating About Abortion by P. Brick and B. Taverner. Morristown, NJ: Planned Parenthood of Greater Northern New Jersey, 2003.

Glencoe Human Sexuality (Teacher Annotated ed.) by M. Bronson. Woodland Hills, CA: Glencoe/McGraw Hill, 2009.

"Going Beyond Lecturing by Using Student Web Site Presentations in a Human Sexuality Course" by J. L. Hughes. *American Journal of Sexuality Education*, 3(4), 387–398.

Guidelines for Comprehensive Sexuality Education: Kindergarten through 12th Grade (3rd ed.) by the National Guidelines Task Force. New York: Fulton Press, 2004. www2.gsu.edu/~wwwche/Sex%20ed%20class/guidelines.pdf

Helping Teens Handle Tough Experiences by J. R. Nelson and S. Kjos. Minneapolis: Search Institute Press, 2008.

Interim Report of the National Consensus Process on Sexual Health and Responsible Sexual Behavior by C. Thrasher. Atlanta: Morehouse School of Medicine, 2006.

Making Sense of Abstinence: Lessons for Comprehensive Sex Education by B. Taverner and S. Montfort. Morristown, NJ: Planned Parenthood of Greater Northern New Jersey, 2005.

National Health Education Standards: Achieving Excellence (2nd ed.) by the Joint Committee on National Health Education Standards. Atlanta, GA: The American Cancer Society, 2007.

Older, Wiser, Sexually Smarter: 30 Sex Ed Lessons for Adults Only by P. Brick, J. Lundquist, A. Sandak, and B. Taverner. Morristown, NJ: Planned Parenthood of Greater Northern New Jersey, 2009.

Our Whole Lives: Sexuality Education for Grades 7–9 by P. M. Wilson. Boston: Unitarian Universalist Association, 1999.

Our Whole Lives: Sexuality Education for Grades 10–12 by E. S. Goldfarb and E. M. Casparian. Boston: Unitarian Universalist Association, 2000.

Promoting Sexual Responsibility: A Teen Pregnancy Prevention Resource for School Employees by E. Marx, V. Harrison, and K. S. Riggs. Washington, D.C.: National Education Association, 2005.

Reducing Adolescent Sexual Risk: A Theoretical Guide for Developing and Adapting Curriculum-Based Programs by Douglas Kirby, et al. Scotts Valley, CA: ETR Associates, 2011.

Reducing the Risk: Building Skills to Prevent Pregnancy STD & HIV (4th ed.) by R. P. Barth. Scotts Valley, CA: ETR Associates, 2004.

Science and Success: Sex Ed and Other Programs That Work to Prevent Teen Pregnancy, HIV and Sexually Transmitted Infections (2nd ed.) by Advocates for Youth. Washington, D.C.: Advocates for Youth, 2008. www2.gsu.edu/~wwwche/ Sex%20ed%20class/guidelines.pdf

Sexuality Education: Theory and Practice (5th ed.) by C. Bruess and J. Greenberg. Sudbury, MA: Jones and Bartlett Publishers, 2009.

The Surgeon General's Call to Action to Promote Sexual Health and Responsible Sexual Behavior by the Office of the Surgeon General. Washington, D.C.: U.S. Government Printing Office, 2001.

Streetwise to Sex-Wise: Sexuality Education for High-Risk Youth (2nd ed.) by S. Brown and B. Taverner. Morristown, NJ: Planned Parenthood of Greater Northern New Jersey, 2001.

Teaching About Sexuality and HIV: Principles and Methods of Effective Education by E. Hedgepeth and J. Helmich. New York: New York University Press, 1996.

This We Believe: Keys to Educating Young Adolescents by the National Middle School Association. Westerville, OH: NMSA, 2010.

Tool to Assess the Characteristics of Effective Sex and STD/HIV Education Programs by D. Kirby, L. A. Rolleri, and M. M. Wilson. Washington, D.C.: Healthy Teen Network, 2007.

General Teaching

The Best of Building Assets Together: Favorite Group Activities That Help Youth Succeed by J. L. Roehlkepartain. Minneapolis: Search Institute Press, 2008.

Connecting in Your Classroom: 18 Teachers Tell How They Foster the Relationships That Lead to Student Success by N. Starkman. Minneapolis: Search Institute Press, 2006.

Engage Every Student: Motivation Tools for Teachers and Parents by E. Kirby and J. McDonald. Minneapolis: Search Institute Press, 2009.

Get Things Going: 85 Asset-Building Activities for Workshops, Presentations, and Meetings by Susan Ragsdale and Ann Saylor. Minneapolis: Search Institute Press, 2011.

Great Places to Learn (2nd ed.) by N. Starkman, P. C. Scales, and C. Roberts. Minneapolis: Search Institute Press, 2006.

How Was Your *Day at School? Improving Dialogue about Teacher Job Satisfaction* by N. Eklund. Minneapolis: Search Institute Press, 2008.

Ideas for Educators: 42 Ready-to-Use Newsletters for School Success by N. Eklund and A. Gilby. Minneapolis, MN: Search Institute Press, 2009.

The Kid's Guide to Service Projects by B. A. Lewis. Minneapolis, MN: Free Spirit Publishing Inc., 1995 (pp. 60–76).

Pass It On at School!: Activity Handouts for Creating Caring Schools by J. Engelmann. Minneapolis: Search Institute Press, 2003.

YOU: The Psychology of Surviving and Enhancing Your Life by S. Gordon and R. Conant. New York: Strawberry Hill with The *New York Times* Book Comp, 1975.

Child and Adolescent Development

All Kids Are Our Kids (2nd ed.) by P. L. Benson. San Francisco: Jossey-Bass, 2006.

Changing Bodies Changing Lives (3rd ed.) by R. Bell. New York: Three Rivers Press, 1998.

Developing Adolescents: A Reference for Professionals by the American Psychological Association. Washington, D.C.: APA, 2002. www2.gsu.edu/~wwwche/Sex%20 ed%20class/guidelines.pdf

Developmental Assets: A Synthesis of the Scientific Research on Adolescent Development (2nd ed.) by P. C. Scales and N. Leffert. Minneapolis: Search Institute Press, 2004.

What Teens Need to Succeed by P. L. Benson, J. Galbraith, and P. Espeland. Minneapolis: Free Spirit Publishing Inc., 1998.

You Can Make a Difference for Kids by E. C. Roehlkepartain. Minneapolis: Search Institute Press, 1997.

Law

The Constitution of the United States

Religious Freedom and the Supreme Court by R. B. Flowers, M. Rogers, and S. K. Green. Waco, TX: Baylor University Press, 2008 (pp. 11–63).

That Godless Court? by R. B. Flowers. Louisville, KY: Westminster John Knox Press, 1994 (pp. 81–102).

For Youth

Boy's Guide to Becoming a Teen by the American Medical Association. San Francisco: Jossey-Bass, 2006.

Girl's Guide to Becoming a Teen by the American Medical Association. San Francisco: Jossey-Bass, 2006.

It's NOT the Stork! by R. H. Harris. Somerville, MA: Candlewick Press, 2006.

It's Perfectly Normal: Changing Bodies, Growing Up, Sex, and Sexual Health by R. H. Harris. Somerville, MA: Candlewick Press, 2004.

It's So Amazing by R. H. Harris. Somerville, MA: Candlewick Press, 2002.

S.E.X.: The All-You-Need-To-Know Progressive Sexuality Guide to Get You Through High School and College by H. Corinna. Philadelphia: Da Capo Press, 2007.

Sexual Etiquette 101 & More by R. A. Thatcher, S. Colestock, E. I. Pluhar, and C. Thrasher. Dawsonville, GA: Bridging the Gap Communications, Inc., 2002.

Succeed Every Day: Daily Readings for Teens by P. Espeland. Minneapolis, MN: Free Spirit Publishing Inc., 2003.

"Where Did I Come From?" by P. Mayle. New York: Lyle Stuart, 1987.

For Parents

All Families Are Different by S. Gordon. Amherst, NY: Prometheus Books, 2000.

Beyond the Big Talk by D. W. Haffner. New York: Newmarket Press, 2002.

Emotional Intelligence: Why It Can Matter More Than IQ (10th ed.) by D. Goleman. New York: Bantam, 2006

From Diapers to Dating: A Parent's Guide to Raising Sexually Healthy Children by D. W. Haffner. New York: Newmarket Press, 2000.

P.E.T. Parent Effectiveness Training by T. Gordon. New York: The Penguin Group, 1975.

Raising a Child Responsibly in a Sexually Permissive World (2nd ed.) by S. Gordon and J. Gordon. Holbrook, MA: Adams Media Corporation, 2000.

The Secret Lives of Teen Girls: What Your Mother Wouldn't Talk about but Your Daughter Needs to Know by E. Resh. Carlsbad, CA: Hay House, Inc., 2009.

Sex & Sensibility: The Thinking Parent's Guide to Talking Sense About Sex by D. Roffman. New York: Perseus Publishing, 2008.

What Every 21st-Century Parent Needs to Know: Facing Today's Challenges with Wisdom and Heart by D. W. Haffner. New York: Newmarket Press, 2008.

Why Do Men Have Nipples? by M. Leyner and B. Goldberg. New York: Three Rivers Press, 2005.

DVDs for Parents and/or Students

Let's Talk About Sex: A Film by James Houston. New Video. 2011. www.letstalkaboutsexthefilm.com

Daddy I Do: Until Marriage Do We Part. Jaye Bird Productions. 2010.

Professional Organizations

My experience with the following organizations began by attending their national conferences and working with their local or regional groups. It made a big difference in my ability to stay focused on the educational discipline of sex education. The people I met and networked with made the difference for me between teaching from a basic health textbook and including the state-of-the-art sexuality education being taught around the country. Teaching can be a lonely occupation if you never get out of the classroom. Join some organizations and participate! Here are a few that helped me (listed alphabetically):

AAHE

American Association for Health Education

www.aahperd.org/aahe

Although you can get lost inside the huge sponsoring organization, AAHPERD, the American Association for Health, Physical Education, Recreation, and Dance, AAHE can be a great resource.

AASECT

American Association of Sexuality Educators, Counselors, and Therapists

AASECT.org

In the early years of teaching, the conferences introduced me to the topics and the people in the field. It continues to be a great resource with a lively listserv.

American Journal of Sexuality Education

www.tandf.co.uk/journals/titles/15546128.asp

For under $100 a year, teachers can subscribe to this great online journal, read current articles and lesson plans from people around the country, and even go back in time to catch up on back issues. Overall, a great buy. There is a discount for membership in some organizations.

ASHA

American School Health Association

www.ashaweb.org

ASHA feels like a small supportive organization with people who are committed to comprehensive sex education, even though it is large. *The Journal of School Health* is published through this organization, and there is a place where teaching techniques are highlighted. Great annual national conference.

SSSS

The Society of the Scientific Study of Sexuality

www.sexscience.org

Educators are welcome here, and there are many opportunities for professional growth and leadership. The feel of this organization is different. It is inclusive and focused on sexuality issues.

There are many more organizations that may support your work in sex education better than the ones I named. Go online and ask around. You might even want to start your own support group. I joined an informal group in the early '80s that started meeting annually for a weekend retreat, and we have grown up together in the field of sexuality, helping each other through the tough times and celebrating our successes. We have created a listserv and can ask each other questions daily.

Websites for Professionals

www.advocatesforyouth.org
One of my top three choices. There is something for everyone here. This organization is on top of political action as well as the pedagogy of sex education.

answer.rutgers.edu
Complete go-to resource for teachers seeking information about sex education by a national advocacy group.

www.cdc.gov/healthyyouth/sexualbehaviors/index.htm
Another winning website from CDC.

www.cdc.gov/yrbs
Home for the Youth Risk Behavior Surveillance from the Centers for Disease Control and Prevention. The trends section of the YRBS is extremely useful.

www.etr.org/recapp
Amazing sex ed lessons—all topics.

www.glsen.org
Gay, Lesbian & Straight Education Network. A must for teachers and families.

honestexchange.com
Valuable resource for sex educators.

www.itsyoursexlife.com
MTV offers health and sex education here, which includes episodes and discussion guides for classes.

www.iwannaknow.org
Kids' site of the American School Health Association.

www.not-2-late.com
Princeton University website on the morning-after pill. For teachers.

www.plannedparenthood.org
Planned Parenthood information about relationship education as well as services.

religiousinstitute.org
Learn how to talk about religion and sexuality.

www.scarleteen.com
Real answers—all the answers—for young people.

www.search-institute.org
This is the place to learn what every kid needs to grow into a healthy, productive, caring, and responsible adult.

www.sexedlibrary.org
Professional resource from SIECUS, Sexuality Information and Education Council of the United States. Great lesson plans.

www.siecus.org
Official website for SIECUS, the Sexuality Information and Education Council of the United States. Endless support here.

www.teenpregnancy.org
Great source for data about sex education sponsored by the National Campaign to Prevent Teen and Unplanned Pregnancy.

www.universityassociates.com
This is the place to learn group facilitation skills.

Websites for Teens

www.seriouslysexuality.org
This is the site sponsored by SIECUS (Sexuality Information and Education Council of the United States)—comprehensive yet basic and polite.

www.plannedparenthood.org/info-for-teens
Planned Parenthood has a section for teens where they can search for answers themselves or ask the experts. Way more on abstinence than abortion.

www.sexetc.org
Sexetc.org is by teens for teens, sponsored by Answer, a national sex education advocacy group.

www.kidshealth.org
Some of my students like this website because it's easy to use and has an audio component that reads the text.

www.itsyoursexlife.com
Itsyoursexlife.com is the official website of MTV and the Kaiser Family Foundation's Emmy Award–winning It's Your (Sex) Life public information campaign.

stayteen.org
The National Campaign to Prevent Teen and Unplanned Pregnancy created this site to coordinate with MTV's show *16 and Pregnant*.

www.iwannaknow.org
The American School Health Association website targets not only health and sexuality education, but also has more links to other sex ed sites.

www.scarleteen.com
Heather Corinna shares detailed information and answers questions that teens need to know about themselves and their relationships. She also has a text hotline.

www.rainn.org
This is a site to support victims of rape, abuse, and incest.

www.goaskalice.columbia.edu
This is Columbia University's sexual health website for their student population, but younger people will want to see this site.

www.cdc.gov

The home page of the Centers for Disease Control and Prevention has a healthy living section and includes information about sexuality.

www.glsen.org

Gay, Lesbian, and Straight Education Network. This is a good source for information, support, and videos.

www.amplifyyourvoice.org/youthresource

Advocates for Youth supports this website for GLBT youth.

Index

About the Author

A nationally known health and sexuality educator, **Martha R. Roper** has degrees from Texas Christian University and Columbia University Teachers College. A teacher for 40 years, she has taught high school health in the School District of University City and Parkway School District in the St. Louis, Missouri, area since 1974. She has taught teachers in local universities and has spoken to parent groups in the St. Louis area. Her course in human sexuality has been named one of the top 10 U.S. sexuality education programs, listed in *Who's Who Among America's Teachers*, and featured in *Parents* magazine, *USA Today*, *CBS Sunday Morning*, and a widely noted ABC-TV special on AIDS, hosted by Peter Jennings, among many other appearances. Roper was a regular guest on KMOX Radio in St. Louis for 15 years. A member of the groundbreaking National Sexuality Education Guidelines Task Force, she was also named the National Health Education Professional of the Year. She and her husband, Dr. Peter C. Scales, jointly received the Lifetime Professional Service Award from Planned Parenthood of the Greater St. Louis Area.